The author and his wife, Militza-Jane,
at Ménage à Trois Restaurant,
Knightsbridge.

THE
SMALL AND
BEAUTIFUL
COOKBOOK

SECRETS OF THE
MÉNAGE À TROIS
RESTAURANT

ANTONY
WORRALL–THOMPSON

Photographs by Bryce Attwell

WEIDENFELD AND NICOLSON · LONDON

To all the young ladies in my past and to MILITZA-JANE, my present and future ....

Text © Antony Worrall-Thompson 1984
Photographs © Bryce Attwell 1984
Reprinted 1985
First paperback edition 1985

Editor Jane Lunzer
Designed by Sara Komar

George Weidenfeld & Nicolson Limited
91 Clapham High Street, London sw4 7TA

Casebound ISBN 0 297 78506 0
Paperback ISBN 0 297 78747 0

Filmset by Keyspools Limited, Golborne, Lancashire
Colour separations by Newsele Litho Ltd, Milan
Printed and bound in Italy by L.E.G.O., Vicenza

CONTENTS

INTRODUCTION

In November 1981 I created a stir among the conventional London restaurant world by opening the Ménage à Trois, a restaurant serving only 'starters' and puddings. Most people dismissed it as a passing gimmick, but three years have now passed and not only is the restaurant still open but it is an unqualified success.

The idea came to me as a result of dining on many occasions with various ladies who, almost without exception, would say 'I wish I could just have a couple of starters'. Invariably the waiter would make it clear that this was unacceptable. There was clearly an opportunity to be taken if it could be tackled in the right way. I determined to create exciting dishes based on two important principles: the produce must be of the highest standards and the finished dishes must be appealing to the eye as well as to the palate – principles to which all good cooks must adhere.

From eating in many of the best restaurants I had noticed that, although the food was excellent, very few people seemed to be relaxed. I questioned the possible reasons: was it the decor? I decided to have pretty, feminine surroundings; was it the lack of music? I introduced a pianist to promote a relaxed, club-like atmosphere; was there something in the attitude of the waiters that unnerved customers? I employed young, attractive and intelligent girls who made the customers feel welcome. I felt too that the stuffiness of traditional wine lists could be intimidating, so with the help of my friend and head barman, Eddie Khoo, we introduced amazing cocktails and a large variety of moderately-priced wines. Having flouted the conventions of established dining to such an extent I decided that in some areas I should adopt a traditional approach and carry it out with impeccable attention to detail: crisp white table linen, beautiful flowers, delicate glassware and sparkling silver. The result has been a restaurant full of cheerful people and, even more gratifying, a place where women happily entertain one another.

This book contains recipes for many of the most successful and exciting dishes we have created for the restaurant. Use them and the accompanying photographs to fire your imagination. Have fun experimenting with different combinations: as your confidence grows, so will your cooking ability.

Finally, there are several people who deserve my thanks: Donald and Annie Foster-Firth helped me set up Ménage à Trois; Jane Lunzer has been a tower of strength and patience in helping me put this book together; Bryce Attwell's photographs have magnificently captured the appearance of the dishes; the cookbooks of Elizabeth David, Jane Grigson, Michel Guérard and Fredy Giradet continually inspire me to better things; Michel and Albert Roux are great chefs who have strived to introduce new produce into this country – without their efforts restaurants in Great Britain would still be years behind those in France; David Wilby and Frank Rourke, chefs at Ménage à Trois, have maintained a high standard of cooking during my frequent absences while writing this book; and finally my wife, Militza-Jane, who suffered numerous trials and tribulations as I tested the recipes at home.

HOW TO USE THIS BOOK

* Quantities for the recipes in this book (when given) are intended as first courses, serving four people. To serve more people, increase all the ingredients proportionately. If, however, you wish to serve the dishes as substantial main courses, only increase the quantity of the main ingredients – the meat, fish or vegetable. Ingredients for sauces and presentation remain the same.

* Look up ingredients in the notes, *pages 149–55*: there may be a substitute for an ingredient you find hard to purchase or too expensive. (Rare produce can be found in certain stores such as Harrods and the larger Sainsburys and it is only a matter of time before most of the ingredients will be readily available up and down the country.) The notes will also give approximate times for blanching vegetables and other useful information.

* Read the list of ingredients and method for the recipe carefully: you will notice that almost all the ingredients require some preparation before assembling the dish. This should be done *earlier in the day*: such work includes making stocks, blanching vegetables, making pastry, boning and trimming meat and fish. Recipes for sauces, dressings, etc., are given at the end of the book, with a page reference given in the main recipe which refers to them.

* This is essentially a cooking of speed; if advance preparation of ingredients has been carried out, most dishes should not take longer than 15 to 20 minutes to complete (apart from soups and cold mousses).

* Half an hour before serving the dish, make the sauce and keep it warm in a bain-marie. Dot the surface with butter or cover it with buttered wax paper to stop a skin forming.

* Times given are approximations. Who am I to tell you how you should cook your meat, fish or vegetables? I know how I like them cooked, but this may not be to your taste.

* Temperatures given are also merely a guide. I cannot judge the efficiency or correctness of your oven or burners; therefore I specify only low (275°–325°F; 140°–170°C; gas mark 1–3), medium (350°–375°F; 180°–190°C; gas mark 4–5) or high (400°–450°F; 200°–230°C; gas mark 6–8).

* Use the photograph of each dish as another guide; it can be frustrating to read wonderful recipes that inspire you, only to be daunted by not knowing how to present them.

* This is above all 'spontaneous cooking': treat the recipes as suggestions to trigger off inspiration. Substitute sauces and garnishes, experiment with new combinations. May I mention, however, that if at all possible you should decorate your creations only with edible ingredients, avoiding the conventional and unappetizing tomato 'roses' and shellfish heads. Try to make all the items on the plate complement each other.

BASKET OF CRUDITÉS
with homemade Dips

MAIN INGREDIENTS
raw vegetables carrots, cauliflower
florets, young artichokes,
Chinese artichokes, Jerusalem
artichokes, avocado, red
cabbage, celery, celeriac, chicory,
cucumber, fennel, kohlrabi,
button mushrooms, spring
onions, peppers, radishes,
seakale, tomatoes, small turnips

blanched vegetables French beans,
broccoli florets, courgettes, small
leeks, mangetouts, new potatoes,
asparagus, salsify
quail eggs, hard-boiled
gull eggs, hard-boiled

The selection of vegetables does not need to be wide. Arrange them on
salad leaves in a basket or dish and serve with one or both of the
following cold dips:

ANCHOVY DIP
150ml [6fl oz] olive oil
1 small can anchovies
3 cloves garlic, crushed
$\frac{1}{2}$ tsp fresh thyme leaves
$\frac{1}{2}$ tsp chopped fresh ginger
$\frac{1}{2}$ tsp fresh basil, chopped
1 tbsp Dijon mustard
1 tbsp lemon juice
1 egg
2 tsp capers
$\frac{1}{2}$ tsp caster sugar
$\frac{1}{2}$ tsp black pepper

ROUILLE
150ml [6fl oz] olive oil
3 hard-boiled egg yolks
2 raw egg yolks
3 cloves garlic, finely chopped
1 tsp tomato purée
$\frac{1}{2}$ tsp ground ginger
juice of 1 lemon
pinch saffron stamens, soaked in
1 tbsp warm water
$1\frac{1}{2}$ tsp Dijon mustard
$\frac{1}{2}$ tsp cayenne pepper
salt and white pepper

For each dip, combine all the ingredients except the oil in a food
processor or liquidizer. Process until smooth. With the machine
running, add oil in a continuous trickle until the sauce emulsifies.

---

*A colourful and convenient way of serving a large number of people with
something more refreshing than crisps or peanuts.*

Iced Tomato Bisque
with Avocado and Basil Sorbet

MAIN INGREDIENTS

4 slices stale white bread, crusts
   removed
1 tbsp red wine vinegar
4 cloves garlic, chopped
1 tbsp caster sugar
75ml [3fl oz] olive oil
650g [1½lb] tomatoes, peeled and
   seeded
425g [15oz] can tomato juice
6 spring onions, finely chopped
1 medium sized cucumber, peeled
   and chopped
2 sweet red peppers, skinned,
   seeded and chopped
2 tbsp fresh basil, chopped
ice cubes
salt and white pepper

PRESENTATION

4 scoops avocado and basil sorbet,
   page 140
12 fresh basil leaves

---

1 Crumble the bread and place in a liquidizer or food processor. Add the vinegar and blend, then the garlic and caster sugar and blend once again.

---

2 With the liquidizer running slowly, add as much olive oil as the bread will absorb without becoming oily.

---

3 Add the tomatoes, tomato juice, spring onions, cucumber, red peppers and chopped basil. Blend.

---

4 Pass through a strainer and dilute with ice cubes. Season.

---

5 Pour the soup into four cold soup bowls, adding a scoop of avocado and basil sorbet and decorating with basil leaves.

For a similar colour contrast, try avocado soup with tomato sorbet.

Mousse of Crab
with Pickled Cucumber and a Tomato Coulis

MAIN INGREDIENTS
½ cucumber, very finely sliced
2 tbsp chilli vinegar
2 tbsp dill weed, chopped
1 tbsp caster sugar
white crab meat, cooked, from a
  1.5kg [3lb] crab
4 crab mousses, cold, made with
  the brown crab meat, *page 141*

SAUCE
200ml [8fl oz] fresh tomato coulis
  with chopped dill added, *page 148*

PRESENTATION
2 tomatoes, peeled, seeded and cut
  into diamond shapes
4 cucumber 'barrels'
chopped chives

---

1 Soak the cucumber in vinegar, dill weed and sugar for at least 20 minutes.

---

2 Sift through the white crab meat and remove any bits of shell.

---

3 Drain the cucumber.

---

4 Turn the crab mousses on to four chilled plates, and place the white crab meat on top of the mousses.

---

5 Pour tomato coulis around the mousses, and cover the sides of the mousses and the tomato coulis with overlapping slices of cucumber. Decorate.

Drain the cucumber slices well, or pat them with absorbent paper. Juices running into the sauce tend to dilute it and make it taste somewhat insipid.

Salad of Raw Scallops with Mango, Melon and Mangetouts and a Sesame Oil Dressing

MAIN INGREDIENTS
12 scallop corals, whole
2 tbsp dry white wine
12 fresh scallops, in thin slices
25g [1oz] pickled ginger, julienned
100g [4oz] mangetouts, blanched
1 small Ogen or Charentais melon,
  scooped into balls with a
  parisienne cutter
1 mango, peeled and julienned
2 tomatoes, peeled, seeded and
  julienned
salt and white pepper

DRESSING
150ml [6fl oz] sesame oil dressing,
  page 146

PRESENTATION
4 asparagus tips, cooked and
  halved lengthways

---

1 Blanch the scallop corals for 1 minute in dry white wine, and allow to cool. Marinate the scallops with the pickled ginger for 20 minutes.

---

2 Drain the scallops and ginger to remove all pickling solution. Season.

---

3 Toss all main ingredients in sesame oil dressing.

---

4 Divide between four cold plates. Decorate with the asparagus.

Poach the scallops for a minute or two if eating them raw does not appeal. This should be done after marinating.

HANBURY YOLK
Poached Egg served on an Artichoke with Seafood and a Smoked Cod's Roe Sauce

MAIN INGREDIENTS

4 artichoke bottoms, cooked
4 eggs, soft-poached
2 scallops, shelled and halved
  horizontally
4 langoustines, cooked and shelled
1 lobster tail, cooked and cut into 4
  medallions
4 × 10g [½oz] Scotch smoked
  salmon rolls
4 oysters, shelled
8 mussels, cooked and shelled
50g [2oz] Sevruga caviar

SAUCE

300ml [12fl oz] cold smoked cod's
  roe sauce, *page 147*

PRESENTATION

4 cherry tomatoes, peeled
4 broccoli florets, cooked
8 mangetouts, blanched
1 tsp salmon eggs, soaked in cold
  water

---

1 Divide three-quarters of the sauce between four chilled plates.

---

2 Place an artichoke bottom on each and top this with a cold poached egg.

---

3 Spoon a little of the remaining sauce over the eggs, and place one each of the different fish on top, leaving the caviar until last.

---

4 Decorate with tomatoes, broccoli, mangetouts and salmon eggs.

A favourite dish of Marika Hanbury-Tenison to whom it is dedicated.

Josephine's Delight
Trio of Mousses with Caviar Smoked Salmon and Scallops

MAIN INGREDIENTS

12 half egg shells, rinsed and dried
(use four of the eggs for the
creamed egg mousse)
150g [6oz] creamed egg mousse,
page 142
25g [1oz] Beluga caviar
150g [6oz] smoked salmon mousse,
page 147
100g [4oz] Scotch smoked salmon,
diced
150g [6oz] cold scallop mousse,
page 146
2 scallops, diced and marinated in
lime juice
1 tsp chives, chopped

PRESENTATION

salad leaves
lemon wedges

1 Fill four egg shells with creamed egg mousse and top with caviar.

2 Fill four egg shells with smoked salmon mousse and top with diced
smoked salmon.

3 Fill four egg shells with scallop mousse and top with diced scallop
and chives.

4 Decorate with salad leaves. Serve with lemon wedges.

*Inspired by Michel Guérard. If Josephine's extravagance seems a little too
much, fill the egg shells with any mousse or delight and top with sieved egg
yolk or egg white.*

Colchester Oysters and Caviar with poached Quail Eggs and a Sour Cream Dressing

MAIN INGREDIENTS

12 Colchester oysters, shelled:
    retain deeper half of shell
24 quail eggs, soft-poached in
    acidulated water
50g [2oz] Sevruga caviar

SAUCE

150ml [6fl oz] sour cream dressing,
    page 147

PRESENTATION

seaweed
1 hard-boiled egg yolk, sieved
1 tsp chives, chopped
ice cubes

---

1 In each dish place three oyster shells on a bed of ice and seaweed.

---

2 On each shell put two quail eggs and coat them with a small amount of dressing.

---

3 Top with the oysters and caviar. Sprinkle with sieved egg and chives.

The oysters can be poached, or other shellfish used as a substitute.

Patchwork of Salmon and Sea Bass with a Beef Tartare and Coriander

MAIN INGREDIENTS

125g [5oz] fillet of Scotch beef,
  finely chopped but not minced
1 shallot, very finely chopped
1 tsp coriander leaves, finely
  chopped
1 raw egg yolk
$\frac{1}{2}$ tsp Dijon mustard
$\frac{1}{2}$ tsp caster sugar
5 tbsp virgin olive oil
juice of $\frac{1}{2}$ lemon
dash Worcester sauce
dash Tabasco
125g [5oz] fillet of fresh Scotch
  salmon, skinned
125g [5oz] fillet of sea bass, skinned
1 tbsp olive oil
juice of 1 lime
rock salt and black pepper

PRESENTATION

2 hard-boiled egg yolks, chopped
1 tsp chives, chopped
1 tbsp salmon eggs
16 coriander leaves

1 Make a tartare by mixing the beef with chopped shallot and
   coriander leaves.

2 Make a mayonnaise-type dressing by mixing together egg yolk,
   mustard and sugar. Gradually add the olive oil drop by drop. Season
   with lemon juice, Worcester sauce, Tabasco, salt and pepper. Add
   as much dressing to meat as desired.

3 Slice the fish fillets into fine, almost transparent strips. Arrange
   carefully in a patchwork pattern around four chilled plates. Paint
   the fish with a fine coating of olive oil and sprinkle with lime juice.
   Place the beef in the middle of the plates, and surround it with
   chopped egg yolk. Decorate with chives, salmon eggs and
   coriander. Serve with rock salt and black pepper.

*The demand for raw fish becomes greater each week: one of the next
restaurant trends may well be towards Westernized Japanese food.*

ROULADE OF RAW SALMON AND TURBOT with a Spinach Cream and Mint

MAIN INGREDIENTS

2 × 100g [4oz] Scotch salmon
  fillets, skinned and flattened
2 tbsp dill weed, chopped
1 tbsp aquavit
50g [2oz] caster sugar
2 × 100g [4oz] turbot fillets,
  skinned and flattened
juice of 1 lime
200g [8oz] fresh spinach leaves,
  blanched, central rib removed
salt and white pepper

SAUCE

300ml [12fl oz] cold spinach
  cream, *page 147*

PRESENTATION

4 tomatoes, peeled, seeded and
  diced
1 tbsp mint, chopped

---

1 Earlier in the day, marinate the salmon in the dill, aquavit, sugar, salt and pepper.

---

2 One and a half hours ahead, marinate the turbot in lime juice, salt and pepper.

---

3 Make two sandwiches of spinach leaves between turbot and salmon. Trim the edges and roll up like Swiss rolls. Wrap the rolls tightly in foil to keep them in shape, and refrigerate for 1 hour.

---

4 Cut through the foil rolls producing a total of twelve slices. Remove the foil. Spoon spinach cream on to chilled plates. Arrange three slices of fish roulade on each plate and decorate with the tomato and chopped mint.

Raw fish may seem daunting, but the texture in this dish is similar to that of smoked salmon.

Nest of Smoked Salmon and Leeks
with soft-boiled Quail Eggs
and a Smoked Cod's Roe Sauce

MAIN INGREDIENTS
2 leeks, julienned and cooked
150g [6oz] Scotch smoked salmon,
  cut in fine strips
2 tbsp walnut oil dressing, *page 149*
16 quail eggs, soft-boiled

SAUCE
150ml [6fl oz] cold smoked cod's
  roe sauce, *page 147*

PRESENTATION
1 tsp chives, chopped

1 Make four nests of leek julienne and smoked salmon strips,
   spooning a little dressing over the top of each.

2 Place four eggs on each of the four nests. Top with smoked cod's roe
   sauce and sprinkle with chives.

PAPER-THIN RAW BEEF
with Rock Salt and Colchester Oysters

MAIN INGREDIENTS

325g [12oz] Scotch beef fillet,
   divided into four equal pieces and
   flattened
12 Colchester oysters, shelled:
   reserve strained oyster juices
rock salt

SAUCE

150ml [6fl oz] dill mayonnaise,
   page 142: peel of lemons used in
   making mayonnaise should be
   kept for decoration

PRESENTATION

peel of 2 lemons, julienned and
   blanched
sprigs of dill weed

1 Spread the paper-thin pieces of beef on four cold plates. Sprinkle
   with salt crystals.

2 Place three oysters on each piece of beef, and sprinkle with a little
   strained oyster juice. Decorate the oysters with lemon peel and dill
   sprigs. Serve the dill mayonnaise separately.

The textures of these raw ingredients are the attraction of the dish.

WHOLE POACHED PEAR
with a Leek and Roquefort Mousse
and a Watercress Cream

MAIN INGREDIENTS
4 Comice pears, peeled and
  poached
150g [6oz] leek and Roquefort
  mousse, *page 144*
1 leek, julienned and cooked

SAUCES
300ml [12fl oz] cold watercress
  cream, *page 149*
4 tbsp cold Roquefort cream,
  page 146

PRESENTATION
1 bunch watercress, washed and
  dried
2 tbsp walnut oil dressing, *page 149*

1 Core each pear, starting from the base and leaving the stalks
   attached.

2 Pipe the hollows full of mousse and put a little mousse in the centre
   of each of the four chilled plates for the pears to stand on.

3 Put one pear in the middle of each plate and surround it with leek
   julienne and watercress cream.

4 Trickle Roquefort cream over the pears.

5 Dip the watercress leaves into the walnut oil dressing and arrange
   them around the edge of each plate.

Chilled Leek with Wild Mushrooms and a Dill Cream

MAIN INGREDIENTS
4 young leeks, cooked, refreshed,
    drained and seasoned
200g [8oz] wild mushroom duxelle,
    page 142

SAUCE
150ml [6fl oz] cold dill cream,
    page 142

PRESENTATION
sprigs of dill weed

Arrange as shown in the photograph.

Increases the interest of a leek quite remarkably.

MOUSSE of JERUSALEM ARTICHOKES with a Salad of Mussels and Vegetables

MAIN INGREDIENTS
450g [1lb] Dutch mussels
150ml [6fl oz] dry white wine
2 shallots, chopped
2 cloves garlic, chopped
1 bay leaf
450g [1lb] Jerusalem artichokes
3 leaves gelatine
150ml [6fl oz] double cream
3 egg whites
2 globe artichoke bottoms, cooked
    and diced
2 tomatoes, peeled, seeded and
    diced
4 spring onions, cut into 2cm
    [1 inch] lengths
salt and white pepper

DRESSING
150ml [6fl oz] walnut oil dressing,
    page 149

PRESENTATION
fresh herbs

---

1 Wash the mussels thoroughly and, adding the wine, shallots, garlic and bay leaf, cover and cook until open. Shell and allow to cool. Discard any that have not opened. Reserve the cooking liquid.

---

2 Peel and slice the Jerusalem artichokes and simmer for 15 minutes in plenty of mussel stock and water.

---

3 Soften the gelatine in a third of the cream. Drain the artichokes, and purée them while still warm with the gelatine mixture. Season, turn out into a bowl and allow to cool.

---

4 Whip the remaining cream to soft peaks. In a separate bowl whip the egg whites to a similar consistency. Fold the whipped cream and then the whipped egg whites into the Jerusalem artichoke purée.

---

5 Add the mussels to the purée and put the mixture into one large mould or several smaller ones. Refrigerate for 2 hours.

---

6 Toss the artichoke bottoms, tomatoes and spring onions lightly in the dressing.

---

7 Dip the moulds in hot water for 3 seconds, and turn the mousses out on to cold plates. Surround the mousses with the vegetables and decorate.

Salad of Smoked Chicken and Lobster with a Walnut Oil Dressing

MAIN INGREDIENTS

½ cucumber, peeled, seeded and cut
   into sticks
julienned cucumber peel
4 spring onions, cut to the same
   length as cucumber sticks
1 head chicory, julienned just
   before use
3 tomatoes, peeled, seeded and
   julienned
julienne of blanched lemon rind:
   use lemon juice for the dressing
1 smoked chicken breast, skinned,
   boned and julienned
450g [1lb] lobster tail, cooked,
   shelled and diced
salt and white pepper

DRESSING

150ml [6fl oz] walnut oil dressing,
   page 149

PRESENTATION

1 pear, peeled and poached
2 tomatoes, peeled, seeded and
   diced
corn salad leaves, dipped into
   dressing

---

1 Sprinkle salt over the cucumber sticks. After 30 minutes, drain and
   rinse the cucumber to remove excessive salt. Dry on absorbent
   paper.

---

2 Toss the main ingredients in walnut oil dressing. Season. Divide
   between four small bowls.

---

3 Quarter and core the cooked pear. Slice and arrange round the plate
   with the corn salad (dipped in dressing) and the diced tomato.

---

*Julienne of smoked ham would be just as delicious if the chicken were
unavailable. Try experimenting with different dressings.*

WARM COCKTAIL OF GARDEN VEGETABLES
with a Cold Mousse of Aubergine

MAIN INGREDIENTS
6 medium-sized aubergines
1 shallot, chopped
1 clove garlic, chopped
9 leaves gelatine
400ml [16fl oz] double cream
300ml [12fl oz] cold jellied stock,
  page 144
4 egg whites
salt and paprika

DRESSING
150ml [6fl oz] walnut oil dressing,
  page 149

PRESENTATION
vegetables, trimmed or sliced and
  blanched: choose from
  cauliflower, broccoli, asparagus,
  tomatoes, mangetouts, French
  beans, carrots, cucumber,
  courgettes, artichokes

---

1 Peel the aubergines and keep the skin. Roughly dice the flesh, and cook it in very little water with the shallot and garlic for about 20 minutes or until soft enough to go into the food processor or liquidizer. Purée until smooth.

---

2 Meanwhile: soften seven leaves of gelatine in a third of the cream and add them to the warm purée. Strain through a fine sieve. Season and allow to cool. Soften the remaining gelatine in cold water.

---

3 Simmer the aubergine peel in the jellied stock with the two leaves of gelatine for about 8 to 10 minutes. Reserve the stock, keeping it at room temperature so it cools but does not set. Line four moulds with the aubergine peel and chill.

---

4 Whip the remaining cream to soft peaks. In a separate bowl whip the egg whites to a similar consistency. Fold first the whipped cream and then the whipped egg whites into the purée. Spoon the mixture into moulds and allow to set in the refrigerator for 2 hours.

---

5 After 2 hours dip the moulds in hot water for 10 seconds and turn them out on to a rack. Coat the cold mousses with the stock.

---

6 Warm the vegetables in the dressing, tossing them gently to ensure that they are glazed all over. Season. Place a mousse in the centre of each of the four plates and arrange the vegetables round them. Serve immediately.

Warm Salad of Green Leaves
with Avocado, Quail Eggs and Roquefort

MAIN INGREDIENTS

6 tbsp walnut oil
4 tbsp lardons
3 tbsp croûtons
1 avocado, peeled and sliced
1 artichoke bottom, cooked and
  julienned
12 quail eggs, soft-boiled and
  shelled
150g [6oz] Roquefort, crumbled
50g [2oz] corn salad, washed and
  dried
100g [4oz] curly endive, washed
  and dried
1 head chicory, wiped
50g [2oz] dandelion leaves, washed
  and dried
salt and black pepper

SAUCES

150ml [6fl oz] cold Roquefort
  cream, *page 146*
4 tbsp walnut oil dressing, *page 149*

PRESENTATION

fresh herbs, choose from: chervil,
  chives, nasturtium and basil
1 tomato, peeled, seeded and
  julienned

---

1 Heat the walnut oil. Fry the lardons until crisp, then add the croûtons and cook until golden brown. Drain off three-quarters of the oil. Add the avocado and artichoke. Toss once or twice to combine ingredients. Add eggs and Roquefort, season, and heat until the cheese begins to melt. Drain with a slotted spoon.

---

2 Deglaze the pan with walnut oil dressing. Toss the salad leaves in the warm dressing and arrange between four warm plates. Sprinkle the other ingredients on top. Spoon the Roquefort cream over the salad, and decorate with herbs and tomato. Serve immediately.

These crisp salads with warm dressings are really special, but do not cut corners: make them just before serving.

YOUNG COURGETTES AND THEIR FLOWERS
stuffed with a Wild Mushroom Mousse

MAIN INGREDIENTS
8 small courgettes with flowers
    attached
200g [8oz] wild mushroom
    mousse, *page 149*

SAUCE
300ml [12fl oz] warm wild
    mushroom sauce, *page 149*

PRESENTATION
50g [2oz] unsalted butter, clarified
1 shallot, finely chopped
16 small morels, washed and dried
2 tbsp cognac
4 cherry tomatoes, peeled
salt and black pepper

1 Rinse the inside of the courgette flowers to remove insects. Do not
  soak. Fit a piping bag with a large straight nozzle and fill with
  mushroom mousse.

2 Carefully pipe the courgette flowers four-fifths full of mousse and
  then fold the ends of the petals to enclose the mousse.

3 Steam the courgettes for approximately 10 minutes, just enough to
  cook the mousse without overcooking the courgettes.

4 Heat the butter, add the shallot and cook over gentle heat until
  softened. Add morels and continue to cook over low heat for 5
  minutes. Season.

5 Turn up the heat. Pour in cognac, ignite and burn off all alcohol.
  When the flames have died down, remove the morels and keep
  warm. Strain the pan juices into the sauce.

6 Spoon the sauce on to warm plates. Slice the courgettes lengthways
  to within 1cm [½ inch] of the flower and fan out on the plates.
  Decorate with the morels and tomatoes.

*Treat the flowers carefully; they are delicate and very susceptible to tearing,
or falling off.*

Twice-Cooked Duck Foie Gras with Raspberry Vinegar

MAIN INGREDIENTS

8 slices fresh duck foie gras
4 Savoy cabbage leaves, blanched,
   central rib removed
salt and white pepper

SAUCE

2 tbsp raspberry vinegar
2 tbsp port
5 tbsp golden veal stock, *page 148*
50g [2oz] cold unsalted butter,
   diced

PRESENTATION

1 punnet fresh raspberries

---

1 Heat a large frying pan and add the slices of foie gras. Seal them for 15 seconds on each side. Season.

---

2 Remove four slices and wrap them individually in cabbage leaves. Steam the parcels for 2 minutes. The four slices remaining in the frying pan should be cooked for a further 20 seconds on each side. Remove them and keep warm on kitchen paper.

---

3 Add vinegar and port to the frying pan to loosen sediment on base. Stir to combine. Add the veal stock. Bring to the boil. Season. Stir in cold butter a piece at a time until emulsified.

---

4 Place the unwrapped foie gras slices in the centres of four warm plates and coat with sauce. Top with the cabbage leaf parcels and decorate with raspberries.

The unique flavour of fresh duck foie gras makes any substitute a disappointing second. However, a similar contrast between ingredients can be achieved by using calf's liver or chicken livers as alternatives to the foie gras.

Warm Salad of French Leaves
with Langoustine and Sweetbreads

MAIN INGREDIENTS

4 tbsp lardons
5 tbsp walnut oil
3 tbsp croûtons
75g [3oz] unsalted butter, clarified
200g [8oz] calf's sweetbreads,
    cooked
16 langoustine tails, cooked and
    shelled
fresh herbs: nasturtium, parsley,
    chives, chervil, basil – roughly
    chopped
lemon juice
100g [4oz] corn salad, washed and
    dried
100g [4oz] curly endive, washed
    and dried
50g [2oz] radicchio, washed and
    dried
50g [2oz] dandelion leaves, washed
    and dried
salt and white pepper

DRESSING

150ml [6fl oz] walnut oil dressing,
    page 149

PRESENTATION

12 cherry tomatoes, peeled
1 orange, peeled and segmented

1   Fry the lardons in hot walnut oil for 2 minutes, stirring well. When
    they begin to crisp, add croûtons and fry until golden brown. Drain
    and set aside.

2   At the same time in another pan heat the butter and sauté the
    sweetbreads for 2 to 3 minutes, turning once. Add the langoustine
    tails and a third of the herbs. Toss together, season with pepper and
    lemon juice, remove and drain. Deglaze the pan with the walnut oil
    dressing.

3   Put the salad leaves in a bowl, sprinkle with another third of the
    herbs and some salt and pepper. Mix with a little warm walnut oil
    dressing, enough to coat but not drown them.

4   Divide the salad between four warm plates. Scatter with lardons
    and croûtons. Arrange the langoustine tails and sweetbreads on
    top, and sprinkle with the remaining herbs. Decorate and serve
    immediately.

A Warm Woodland Salad
with Pigeon and Wild Mushrooms

MAIN INGREDIENTS

5 tbsp walnut oil
1 tbsp lardons
3 tbsp croûtons
4 pigeon breasts
75g [3oz] unsalted butter, clarified
1 shallot, chopped
1 clove garlic, chopped
4 oyster mushrooms
50g [2oz] corn salad, washed and
   dried
100g [4oz] curly endive, washed
   and dried
100g [4oz] radicchio, washed and
   dried
salt and white pepper

DRESSING

3 tbsp walnut oil dressing, *page 149*

PRESENTATION

1 orange, peeled and segmented
8 lychees, peeled and stoned

---

1   Heat the walnut oil and fry the lardons in it until starting to crisp.
    Add the croûtons and fry them until golden brown.

---

2   Season the pigeon breasts. Brown them in 25g [1oz] of the butter.
    Roast in a hot oven for 6 minutes.

---

3   Sweat the shallots and garlic in the remaining butter until soft but
    not brown. Add the oyster mushrooms, raise the heat and sauté
    quickly for 1 minute on each side. Season. Drain and keep warm.
    Add the walnut oil dressing to pan and warm.

---

4   Carve the pigeon breasts into thin strips. Toss the salad leaves in
    warm walnut oil dressing and divide between four warm plates.
    Sprinkle lardons and croûtons over the salad and top with pigeon
    strips and oyster mushrooms. Decorate with orange segments and
    lychees. Serve immediately.

Other game birds can be used as substitutes for pigeon.

Filo Pastry 'Frying Pan'
with Wild Mushrooms and Garden Vegetables

MAIN INGREDIENTS

150g [6oz] unsalted butter,
  clarified
8 sheets filo pastry, and another
  2 sheets cut in half horizontally
1 shallot, finely chopped
vegetables, trimmed to similar sizes
  and blanched, from the
  following: young carrots with
  2cm [1 inch] of foliage,
  asparagus tips, mangetouts,
  French beans, broccoli,
  courgettes, young leeks,
  cauliflower

wild mushrooms, washed, dried
  and sliced:
  25g [1oz] chanterelles
  25g [1oz] oyster mushrooms
  25g [1oz] wood hedgehog
  mushrooms
  25g [1oz] horns of plenty
salt and black pepper

SAUCE

300ml [12fl oz] warm wild
  mushroom sauce, *page 149*

PRESENTATION

4 cherry tomatoes, peeled
25g [1oz] truffle, julienned

---

1 To make filo pastry 'frying pans', brush one whole pastry sheet with melted butter and fold in two, see the diagram, *page 138*. Lay it in a small iron frying pan, mould to the shape of the pan, and trim off the excess. Butter a half sheet, roll it up to make a 'handle' and lay it partly in the pan but with 8cm [3 inches] extending up the real pan handle.

---

2 To secure the 'handle', cover the 'pan' area with another sheet, folded. Trim this to shape and prick all over with a fork. Brush once more with butter. Bake, without removing from the real pan, in a hot oven for about 12 minutes, or until crisp and brown.

---

3 Detach the cooked 'pan' gently from the real pan, and make three more 'pans' in the same way.

---

4 Meanwhile, 5 minutes before the last 'pan' is finished, start cooking the vegetables. Add the shallot to the remaining butter and cook in a large frying pan over gentle heat until softened. Increase the heat and add all the mushrooms. Cook for $1\frac{1}{2}$ minutes and then add the other vegetables. Stir-fry until heated through. Season.

---

5 Reheat the pastry 'frying pans' in a warm oven for 3 minutes. Place them gently on plates. When the vegetables are ready, check the seasoning and arrange them in the 'pans'. Top with truffle julienne and tomatoes. Serve the sauce separately.

Warm Salad of Chicory and Corn Salad with Scallops, Tomato and Red Mullet

MAIN INGREDIENTS

4 medium-sized tomatoes, peeled
100g [4oz] corn salad, washed and
   dried
2 heads chicory
½ lemon
8 small red mullet fillets, cut into
   long strips
4 scallops, each shelled and sliced
   into three horizontally
50g [2oz] unsalted butter, clarified
1 tbsp olive oil
salt and white pepper

SAUCE

150ml [6fl oz] cold dill cream mixed
   with 2 tbsp of cold spinach cream,
   pages 142 and 147
2 tbsp hazelnut oil dressing,
   page 143

PRESENTATION

sprigs of dill weed

---

1 Cut the tops off the tomatoes. Scoop out the seeds with a parisienne
   cutter and lightly salt the insides. Turn the tomatoes upside down
   and leave for 30 minutes.

---

2 Pull the chicory leaves apart by hand. (Try not to cut chicory with a
   knife unless it is to be used immediately; it discolours.)

---

3 Rinse the insides of the tomatoes with cold water, drain and fill with
   dill and spinach cream.

---

4 Squeeze the lemon over the red mullet fillets and scallops. Season.
   Sauté the red mullet fillets in butter and oil for 2 minutes, skin side
   down, then turn them over. Add the scallops, cooking for
   20 seconds each side. Remove and keep warm. Deglaze the pan
   with the hazelnut oil dressing.

---

5 Toss the salad leaves in the warm dressing and arrange on four
   warm plates around the tomatoes. Arrange the mullet and scallops
   and decorate with dill. Serve immediately.

Persuade your greengrocer to obtain these delicious Continental salad leaves.

Colchester Oysters
served warm with Spinach and Dill

MAIN INGREDIENTS

16 Colchester oysters, shelled:
   reserve strained oyster juice
1 tbsp dry white vermouth
½ shallot, chopped
16 spinach leaves, blanched,
   drained and central rib removed
200g [8oz] spinach mousse,
   page 147
25g [1oz] unsalted butter, clarified
salt and white pepper

SAUCE

300ml [12fl oz] warm dill sauce,
   page 142

PRESENTATION

2 tsp salmon eggs
8 sprigs of dill weed

---

1 Heat the oyster juices and vermouth with the shallot. Poach the oysters in the liquid for 30 seconds. Allow to cool in the liquid. Use the strained liquid as part of the stock required in the dill sauce.

---

2 Spread out eight spinach leaves. Put a teaspoonful of spinach mousse in the centre of each leaf, and a cooked oyster on top of the mousse. Season. Smooth the mousse around the oyster. Enclose with spinach leaf, squeezing the parcels gently to mould into neat shapes. Steam the parcels for 6 minutes. Steam remaining oysters for 2 minutes.

---

3 Warm the butter and in it heat the remaining spinach leaves. Season.

---

4 Arrange two spinach leaves on each of four warmed plates. Top with the unwrapped oysters and a spoonful of dill sauce. Add two oyster parcels to each plate. Garnish with salmon eggs and fresh dill. Serve the remaining sauce separately.

Dill is the perfect herb for shellfish.

WHOLE MORELS WITH TRUFFLES
and a Morel Sauce

MAIN INGREDIENTS
12 largish and 12 smallish morels,
  washed thoroughly; use stalks
  for mousse
100g [4oz] morel mousse, *page 145*
25g [1oz] unsalted butter, clarified
12 truffle slices (optional)
salt and white pepper

SAUCE
300ml [12fl oz] warm morel sauce,
  page 145
75g [3oz] fresh foie gras, diced

1 Fill the 12 larger morels with the mousse, using a small piping bag.
  Season and steam for approximately 8 minutes. Keep warm.

2 Sauté the smaller morels in butter for approximately 3 minutes,
  tossing regularly. Season. Add the truffle slices and the larger
  morels for last 30 seconds.

3 For the sauce, instead of finishing with butter, fold in the finely
  diced foie gras – it will quickly reduce. Stir from time to time to
  emulsify the foie gras juices with the wild mushroom sauce. Strain.

4 Divide the mushroom sauce between four warm plates. Arrange the
  morels and truffle.

Warm Salad of Lobster and Foie Gras with Red and Green Salads

MAIN INGREDIENTS

1 × 450g [1lb] live lobster
200g [8oz] fresh duck foie gras, cut into 8 slices
200g [8oz] radicchio, washed and dried
200g [8oz] corn salad, washed and dried
salt and black pepper

DRESSING

3 tbsp raspberry vinegar
1 shallot, finely chopped
25g [1oz] cold, unsalted butter, diced

PRESENTATION

1 orange, peeled and segmented
1 punnet raspberries
2 tbsp fresh chopped herbs, choose from: chives, mint, basil, chervil

---

1 Twenty minutes in advance, cook the lobster in a boiling court-bouillon for 10 minutes. Keep it warm in the liquid.

---

2 Season the foie gras slices and fry them in a hot pan for 20 seconds on each side; no extra fat is needed. Put them on kitchen paper and keep warm. Reserve the fat in the pan.

---

3 Shell the lobster and divide the meat from claws and body into four.

---

4 Sweat the shallot in the fat from the foie gras over a low heat. Raise the heat and add the raspberry vinegar, then the butter in small cubes. Stir until emulsified. Toss the salad leaves in this warm dressing. Arrange them on four warm plates.

---

5 Top with lobster and slices of foie gras, and decorate with orange segments, raspberries and herbs.

Trio of Sea Urchins
with Hen, Gull and Quail Eggs

MAIN INGREDIENTS

12 sea urchins
1 shallot
½ clove garlic
25g [1oz] unsalted butter, clarified
4 gull eggs
7 tbsp double cream
4 medium-sized hen eggs
1 tsp grated horseradish
acidulated water

8 quail eggs
450g [1lb] rock salt
salt and black pepper

PRESENTATION

urchin roe
2 tsp chives, chopped
50g [2oz] smoked salmon
25g [1oz] Beluga caviar

1 Cut open the urchins with special cutters or kitchen scissors. Cut off the top with the 'eye', leaving a perfect rounded container. Strain off the juices and the orange roe and reserve both.

2 Clean the urchin shells thoroughly, making quite sure there are no loose spines left inside. Spread the rock salt on four plates and put them and shells to warm in the oven.

3 Sweat the chopped shallot and garlic in butter until soft but not brown. Add three-quarters of the roe and toss gently for 1 minute. Divide this mixture between the twelve shells and return them to the oven while assembling the fillings. Reserve remaining roe for presentation.

4 Break a gull egg carefully on to the roe in four of the shells. Season, and top each with a tablespoon of cream mixed with urchin juice. Bake in medium oven in a bain-marie for about 6 to 8 minutes. Decorate with reserved urchin roe.

5 Scramble hen eggs (use method for scrambled quail eggs on *page 67*). Divide between another four of the roe-filled urchin shells and top with salmon and chives.

6 Poach quail eggs (use method on *page 67*). Place two poached eggs in each of the remaining roe-filled urchin shells and top with a tablespoon of cream mixed with urchin juice. Season and decorate with caviar.

7 Keep the filled urchin eggs warm on the plates of hot rock salt. Serve one of each sort on each of the four plates.

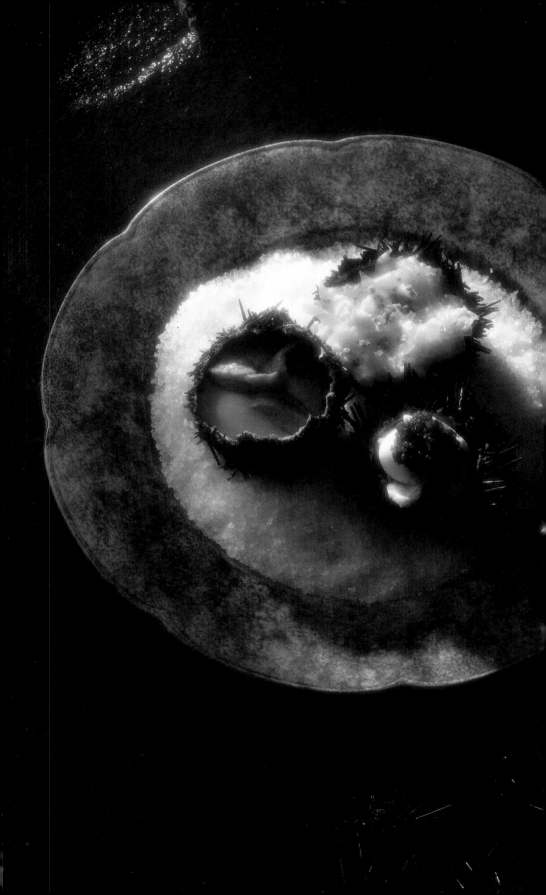

Duck Magret with Oysters and a Champagne Sauce

MAIN INGREDIENTS

16 Colchester oysters, shelled;
 reserve strained oyster juices
8 spinach leaves, blanched and
 central rib removed
150g [6oz] spinach mousse,
 page 147
200g [8oz] duck magret, fatty skin
 removed and diced
salt and black pepper

SAUCES

150ml [6fl oz] warm champagne
 sauce, *page 141*
75ml [3fl oz] walnut oil dressing,
 page 149

PRESENTATION

sprigs of dill weed
2 tomatoes, peeled, seeded and
 quartered

1 Blanch eight of the oysters for 1 minute in their juices. Allow to cool.

2 Spread the spinach leaves over flat surface and place a teaspoonful of spinach mousse in the centre of each. Top with a blanched oyster and a second teaspoonful of mousse. Fold the leaf to enclose the parcel. Steam the parcels for approximately 8 minutes.

3 At the same time, put the duck magret in a roasting tin, scatter the diced skin, season and roast for 8 to 12 minutes. Remove it from the oven and keep the duck warm. Drain the melted fats from the roasting tin and return tin to the oven with the skin in it. When crisp, remove the skin, drain again and deglaze the tin with walnut oil dressing.

4 Heat the champagne sauce and add the remaining eight oysters. Warm through but do not allow to boil. Cut the duck into julienne strips and toss them in the warm walnut oil dressing.

5 Place the duck julienne and crisp skin in centre of warm plates. Arrange the other ingredients and decorate.

English duckling can be used as a substitute for duck magret.

Warm Salad of Dandelion
with Lamb's Kidneys and Chicken Livers

MAIN INGREDIENTS
200g [8oz] chicken livers
4 lamb's kidneys in suet
4 tbsp walnut oil
4 tbsp lardons
3 tbsp croûtons
25g [1oz] unsalted butter, clarified
2 sage leaves
325g [12oz] dandelion leaves,
   washed and dried
salt and black pepper

DRESSING
4 tbsp walnut oil dressing, *page 149*

PRESENTATION
1 bunch watercress, washed and
   drained
4 tomatoes, peeled, seeded and
   quartered
2 oranges, peeled and segmented

---

1 One hour before serving, soak the chicken livers in iced water.

---

2 Twenty minutes before serving, drain and dry the livers. Trim the suet from the kidney leaving a thin covering. Season.

---

3 Cook the kidneys in a hot oven for about 8 to 12 minutes, more if preferred well done. Remove from the oven but keep warm.

---

4 Heat the oil and add the lardons. Cook until starting to crisp, turning regularly. Add the croûtons and cook until golden brown. Drain and keep warm.

---

5 Strain the oil and return it to the pan. Add the butter and heat. Sauté the chicken livers with the sage leaves, turning regularly. Cook for 3 to 5 minutes, season and drain. Remove three-quarters of the juices and add the dressing to the remainder in the pan.

---

6 Toss the dandelion leaves in the warm dressing, and divide on to four warm plates. Sprinkle with lardons and croûtons. Slice the kidneys and arrange on top of the salad with the livers.

---

7 Decorate with watercress, tomato and orange.

Curly endive would be a good substitute for dandelion.

QUAIL EGGS
with Caviar, Smoked Salmon and Truffle

MAIN PRESENTATION
12 round croûtons, 2cm [1 inch]
  diameter
6 cherry tomatoes, peeled and
  halved

1 tsp chives, chopped
12 spinach leaves, blanched and
  central rib removed
3 tbsp leek, julienned and cooked

---

1 SCRAMBLED QUAIL EGGS
  8 quail eggs
  1 tbsp double cream
  10g [$\frac{1}{2}$oz] unsalted butter,
    clarified
  1 tsp grated horseradish
  salt and white pepper

PRESENTATION
50g [2oz] smoked salmon

Heat the butter, cream and horseradish. Crack the eggs into a cup
and break up with a fork. Add the eggs to saucepan and cook to the
right consistency. Season. Keep warm.

---

2 POACHED QUAIL EGGS
  4 quail eggs
  acidulated water, *page 155*

PRESENTATION
2 tbsp horseradish cream, *page 143*
25g [1oz] Beluga caviar

Crack each egg on to a spoon and slide gently into simmering
acidulated water. Cook 1$\frac{1}{2}$ minutes. Drain, trim and keep warm.
When serving, top with horseradish cream.

---

3 FRIED QUAIL EGGS
  4 quail eggs
  25g [1oz] unsalted butter,
    clarified

PRESENTATION
4 slices truffle, julienned

Fry the eggs gently in butter. Season. Drain and keep warm.

---

4 Gently fry the croûtons in the same butter as the fried eggs.

---

5 Arrange the eggs on the croûtons. Decorate each with smoked
   salmon, caviar or truffle, and sprinkle the scrambled and poached
   eggs with chopped chives.

---

6 Arrange on warm plates together with the tomato halves, spinach,
   leek julienne and any remaining smoked salmon.

MÉNAGE À TROIS
Three hot cheesy pastry parcels

MAIN INGREDIENTS
(Makes 24 parcels)
12 sheets filo pastry, each cut into
   two, *page 138*
100g [4oz] unsalted butter,
   clarified

CAMEMBERT AND
CRANBERRY FILLING
Ingredients for each parcel:
1 small piece of Camembert
1 tsp cranberry sauce
pinch of paprika

Place on pastry in above order.

BOURSIN AND SPINACH
FILLING
Ingredients for each parcel:
1 tbsp spinach mousse, *page 147*
1 tsp Boursin

*Fold Boursin into mousse and place
on pastry.*

LEEK AND ROQUEFORT
FILLING
Ingredients for each parcel:
1 tbsp leek and Roquefort mousse,
   page 144, omitting gelatine
1 small cube Roquefort cheese

*Place mousse on pastry and the
cheese on top.*

For assembly into filo pastry parcels, see the diagrams on *page 138*.
Just before serving, plunge them into hot deep fat and fry until crisp
and golden, about 3 minutes. Serve with sauce and decorations of
your own choice. More filling suggestions are on *pages 144–5*.

Cream Soup of Wild Mushrooms with Ravioli of Truffle and Foie Gras

MAIN INGREDIENTS

2 shallots, finely chopped
1 clove garlic, chopped
1 small potato, peeled and diced
25g [1oz] unsalted butter, clarified
wild mushrooms: 50g [2oz] ceps
   50g [2oz] wood hedgehog
   mushrooms
   50g [2oz] chanterelles
   50g [2oz] oyster mushrooms
1 tbsp peanut oil
1 bay leaf
400ml [16fl oz] vegetable stock,
   page 148
300ml [12fl oz] double cream
3 tbsp truffle juice
pinch of grated nutmeg
1 tbsp champagne vinegar
salt and black pepper

PRESENTATION

12 ravioli filled with truffle and foie
   gras, *page 146*
4 morels, quartered and sautéed in
   butter

1 Cook the shallot, garlic and potato in the butter over a low heat.

2 Sweat the mushrooms in the oil in a large pan until they have released all juices. Add shallot, garlic, potato, bay leaf and vegetable stock. Bring to the boil and simmer for 10 minutes.

3 Add the cream and boil for a further 5 minutes. Remove bay leaf. Liquidize, strain and return to the heat. Skim.

4 Add the truffle juice and season with salt, pepper, nutmeg and champagne vinegar. Bring the soup to the boil once more and add the ravioli. Cook for 2 minutes.

5 Divide between four warm bowls and decorate with morels.

Field mushrooms can be used as a substitute in this excellent soup.

MINESTRONE OF SHELLFISH AND VEGETABLES
perfumed with fresh Basil

MAIN INGREDIENTS
½ bottle dry white wine
1 shallot, finely chopped
2 cloves garlic, crushed
2 tbsp finely chopped fresh ginger
450g [1lb] mussels
4 langoustines, live
750ml [1½ pints] vegetable stock,
  page 148
1 carrot, diced
1 spring onion, sliced

1 leek, sliced
a few broccoli florets
a few cauliflower florets
1 artichoke bottom, cooked and
  diced
1 tomato, peeled, seeded and diced
8 scallops, shelled and sliced in
  halves horizontally
1 small bunch basil
1 tbsp basil butter (optional)
salt and black pepper

1 Boil the wine, shallot, garlic and ginger for 3 minutes. Add the
   mussels, cover the pan and cook over a brisk heat until the mussels
   have opened. Strain through a fine sieve and reserve the juice. Shell
   the mussels, discarding any that have not opened.

2 Boil the langoustines in vegetable stock for 2 minutes. Strain the
   liquid into the mussel stock. Shell the langoustines and cut into
   small slices.

3 Boil the mussel liquid and vegetable stock together. Add the carrot
   and spring onion. Cook for 5 minutes. Add the leek, broccoli and
   cauliflower. Cook for another 5 minutes.

4 Add the mussels, artichoke, tomato and langoustines. Season. Bring
   back to the boil, and add the scallops and julienned basil. Serve at
   once. A little basil butter can be added before serving.

Cream Soup of Mussels and Saffron
accompanied by a Julienne of Vegetables

MAIN INGREDIENTS

75g [3oz] unsalted butter, clarified
2 shallots, finely chopped
2 cloves garlic, finely chopped
2 tsp finely chopped fresh ginger
500ml [1 pint] dry white wine
1 tbsp soy sauce
2kg [4lb] mussels, cleaned
1 stick celery, diced
½ small head fennel, diced
white of 1 leek, diced
1 small potato, diced
1 small carrot, diced
500ml [1 pint] fish stock, *page 142*
1 bay leaf

1 sprig thyme
1 pinch saffron stamens, soaked in
   1 tbsp warm water
300ml [12fl oz] double cream
salt, white pepper and grated
   nutmeg

PRESENTATION

1 leek, julienned and blanched
1 carrot, julienned and blanched
1 tomato, peeled, seeded and very
   finely julienned
25g [1oz] unsalted butter

1 Heat the butter in a large saucepan. Add the shallot, garlic and ginger and cook over a low heat until soft but not brown.

2 Remove half the mixture to a second saucepan. Add the wine and soy sauce to the first pan and bring to the boil. Add the mussels and cook, covered, for approximately 5 minutes, shaking the pan at regular intervals. When the mussels have opened, shell them, discarding any that remain firmly closed, and strain their stock into the second saucepan.

3 Add the vegetables from the main ingredients list, the fish stock, bay leaf and thyme to the mussel stock and sweated shallot mixture. Bring to the boil and simmer for approximately 25 minutes or until the vegetables are soft.

4 Remove the bay leaf and thyme. Liquidize the soup and pass through a fine strainer. Return to the heat. Add the saffron stamens. The soup will turn pale yellow. Add the cream, and season with nutmeg, salt and pepper. Do not allow it to boil.

5 Gently heat the mussels and presentation ingredients in a little butter. Serve with the soup in warm bowls.

Cream Soup of Chicken and Watercress with floating Watercress 'Islands'

MAIN INGREDIENTS
750ml [1½ pints] strong chicken
  stock, *page 141*
1 chicken breast, boned and finely
  diced
2 bunches watercress, washed,
  leaves only: use stalks in
  preparation of stock
300ml [12fl oz] double cream
2 egg yolks mixed with 2 tbsp of the
  cream
salt and white pepper

PRESENTATION
1 handful watercress leaves,
  blanched
8 egg whites, with pinch of salt
  added

---

1 Bring the stock to boil and add the chicken. Simmer for 5 minutes.

---

2 Add two bunches of watercress leaves and the cream. Cook for a
   further 1 minute and then liquidize until smooth. Season.

---

3 Whisk the egg whites to stiff peaks and carefully fold in the handful
   of blanched watercress leaves. Poach spoonfuls of egg white in
   lightly salted water, turning once. Remove and drain on absorbent
   paper.

---

4 Re-heat the soup. Add the egg yolks and cream mixture. Do not
   allow it to boil.

---

5 Serve in warm bowls, with floating watercress islands.

Feuilleté of Langoustine and Asparagus with a Minted Orange Sauce

MAIN INGREDIENTS

20 langoustine tails, cooked and shelled
8 asparagus spears of the same length, cooked
4 puff pastry rectangles approximately 6cm × 2cm [2½ inches × 1 inch], cooked
25g [1oz] unsalted butter, clarified
salt and white pepper

SAUCE

300ml [12fl oz] warm minted orange sauce, *page 145*

PRESENTATION

1 tomato, peeled and quartered
1 orange, peeled and segmented
4 sprigs young mint leaves

1　Heat the langoustine tails and asparagus by tossing gently in hot butter, or by steaming, or by poaching in a little fish stock. Season.

2　Re-heat the pastry rectangles in a hot oven for 1 minute. Split them horizontally.

3　Divide the sauce equally between four warmed plates. Put the bottom half of the pastry case on the sauce, and arrange the langoustine on top. Replace the pastry lid. Lay the asparagus spears in a cross beside the feuilleté and brush with clarified butter. Decorate.

For the langoustine, you can substitute king prawns.

FILLETS OF RED MULLET AND TURBOT
with Asparagus and Two Sauces

MAIN INGREDIENTS

8 × 40g [1½oz] fillets of turbot,
    skinned
8 × 40g [1½oz] fillets of red mullet,
    scales removed
8 asparagus tips, blanched
juice of ½ lemon
salt and white pepper

SAUCES

150ml [6fl oz] warm tomato and
    basil sauce, *page 147*
150ml [6fl oz] warm spinach sauce,
    page 147

PRESENTATION

1 small leek, julienned and
    blanched
1 tomato, skinned, seeded and
    diced
25g [1oz] unsalted butter, clarified

---

1   As far as possible the fish fillets should be trimmed to equal lengths.
    Steam fish fillets and asparagus until cooked, 5 to 7 minutes. (Put
    the turbot in the steamer just ahead of the mullet, as its flesh is
    slightly more dense.) Season with salt, pepper and lemon juice.

---

2   Toss the leek julienne in hot butter. Drain and season.

---

3   Spoon the warm sauces on to warm plates, and arrange the
    ingredients as in the photograph.

---

*The small green circles on the plate are thin slices of asparagus – they add
colour to the dish.*

Mosaic of Salmon and Sole
with a Nettle and Sorrel Sauce

MAIN INGREDIENTS

650g [1½lb] Dover sole, skinned and filleted into four

16 spinach leaves, blanched and central rib removed

325g [12oz] fillet of Scotch salmon, skinned

4 squares aluminium foil, buttered

juice of ½ lemon

salt and white pepper

SAUCE

300ml [12fl oz] warm nettle and sorrel sauce, *page 145*

PRESENTATION

2 tsp salmon eggs, soaked in cold water

1 tbsp chives, chopped

1   Cut each of the four sole fillets into four equal strips, season with salt, pepper and lemon juice, and wrap each strip in a blanched spinach leaf. Trim the edges of all sixteen parcels so that they are uniform in shape and size.

2   Cut the salmon fillet into sixteen strips as near as possible the same size as the sole. Season with salt, pepper and lemon juice.

3   Weave four strips of each sort of fish into a square on each of the sheets of buttered foil. Trim.

4   Steam the fish on the foil for 6 to 8 minutes.

5   Pour sauce on to four warm plates. Place the 'mosaics' on top and decorate.

Knot of Scotch Salmon surrounding a Spinach and Dill Mousse with a Pumpkin Sauce

MAIN INGREDIENTS

325g [12oz] fillet of Scotch salmon,
  skinned
juice of ½ lemon
4 squares aluminium foil, buttered
150g [6oz] spinach and dill
  mousse, *page 147*
salt and white pepper

SAUCE

300ml [12fl oz] warm pumpkin
  sauce, *page 146*

PRESENTATION

1 radish, sliced
8 asparagus tips
1 courgette, blanched and sliced
4 broccoli florets, blanched
4 mangetouts, blanched
4 cucumber 'barrels', blanched
25g [1oz] unsalted butter, clarified
  (optional)

1 Cut the salmon fillet into four equal portions lengthways. Trim off
   any dark flesh.

2 Tie each strip of fillet into a loose knot; salmon is very flexible.
   Season with salt, pepper and lemon juice, and place on buttered foil
   squares.

3 Using a piping bag fitted with a star-shaped nozzle, pipe the spinach
   and dill mousse into the hole. Decorate the mousse with slices of
   radish and half an asparagus tip.

4 Steam the fish for about 8 minutes or until the mousse is
   thoroughly cooked. For the last minute of the steaming add the
   seasoned vegetables, or alternatively toss them in butter until they
   are warmed through and drain carefully.

5 Divide the sauce equally between four warm plates. Carefully lift the
   salmon off the foil sheets on to the plates. Decorate with the warm
   vegetables.

Lobster and Scallops
with a Minted Orange Sauce

MAIN INGREDIENTS

1 × 450g [1lb] live lobster
6 scallops with coral, shelled and
    cleaned
25g [1oz] unsalted butter, clarified
salt and black pepper

SAUCE

300ml [12fl oz] warm minted
    orange sauce, *page 145*

PRESENTATION

4 slices truffle
2 tbsp mint, julienned
1 orange, peeled and segmented

1 Cook the lobster 30 minutes in advance, in a court-bouillon, for
   10 minutes. Leave it in the cooking liquid. When it is cool enough
   to handle, shell it, removing the tail in one piece, and divide into
   two. Shell the claws. Keep warm.

2 Cut each scallop in half horizontally, with its coral.

3 Lightly sauté the scallops and corals for 20 seconds on each side in
   the clarified butter. Season, drain and keep warm.

4 Divide the sauce between four warm plates. Distribute the scallops
   (twelve halves) and lobster (two pieces of tail meat and two claws)
   between the plates and decorate with truffle, mint and orange.

*The orange and mint create an exciting taste for shellfish. Try the dish from
time to time with a saffron and ginger sauce.*

FILLETS OF TURBOT
larded with Truffle and
Salmon with a White Truffle Sauce

MAIN INGREDIENTS

50g [2oz] fillet of Scotch salmon,
  skinned
1 small [25g, 1oz] truffle, cut into
  strips
4 × 100g [4oz] fillets of turbot,
  skinned
50g [2oz] unsalted butter, clarified
450g [1lb] fresh spinach, blanched
  and central rib removed
salt and white pepper

SAUCE

300ml [12fl oz] warm white truffle
  sauce, *page 148*

1 Cut the salmon into strips the same size as the truffle.

2 Using a larding needle, thread the salmon and truffle through the
  turbot.

3 Slice each turbot fillet into three steaks. Season and steam for
  approximately 3 minutes.

4 Heat the butter. Toss the spinach in the butter until warmed
  through. Season well, and drain.

5 Divide the spinach between four warm plates. Arrange three pieces
  of turbot on each plate in a triangle, and pour a little warm sauce
  into the middle of each triangle. Serve the remainder of the sauce
  separately.

*Exciting combinations can be developed by larding the turbot with other
products – for example, anchovy and asparagus, or pimento and apple.*

Spinach-Suited Langoustine
with a Cucumber and Mint Sauce

MAIN INGREDIENTS

24 medium-sized langoustine tails,
 cooked and shelled
24 leaves of fresh spinach,
 blanched and central rib
 removed

SAUCE

300ml [12fl oz] warm cucumber
 and mint sauce, *page 142*

PRESENTATION

24 cucumber balls, made with the
 smallest parisienne cutter and
 blanched
24 tiny sprigs of mint

---

1 Wrap each langoustine tail in a spinach leaf, leaving a small piece
   of tail showing.

---

2 Steam the langoustine tails and the cucumber balls for 2 minutes.

---

3 Place an equal amount of warm sauce on four warm plates. Put six
   langoustine tails on each plate, and decorate with cucumber and
   mint.

---

*Courgettes can be used instead of cucumber, and the dish can be varied by
having a selection of shellfish wrapped in spinach.*

Feuilleté of White Crabmeat with Broccoli, Artichoke and Tomato on a Crab and Armagnac Sauce

MAIN INGREDIENTS

50g [2oz] unsalted butter, clarified
1 shallot, chopped
½ clove garlic, chopped
1 spring onion, chopped
½ tsp chopped fresh ginger
white crab meat from 1.5kg [3lb] cooked crab: use brown meat for sauce
4 triangles puff pastry approximately 5cm [2 inches] along each side, cooked
salt and white pepper

SAUCE

300ml [12fl oz] warm crab and armagnac sauce, *page 141*
2 tomatoes, peeled, seeded and diced
2 artichoke bottoms, cooked and diced

PRESENTATION

broccoli florets, blanched

---

1 Heat 25g [1oz] of butter in a pan and gently sweat the shallot, garlic, spring onion and ginger until soft but not brown. Add the crab meat and heat until warmed through. Season.

---

2 Add the diced tomato and artichoke bottoms to the sauce. Heat through.

---

3 Toss the broccoli in the remaining 25g [1oz] of butter until warmed through. Season.

---

4 Re-heat the pastry triangles in a hot oven for 2 minutes. Split them in two horizontally.

---

5 Divide the warm sauce equally between four warm plates. Place the bottom half of the pastry in the centre of the plate, and arrange the crab on top. Top with pastry lids and decorate with broccoli.

I rarely advocate frozen foods, but there are several excellent brands of frozen crab meat which would turn this into a quick supper dish.

Galaxy of Seasonal Seafood
with a Champagne and Cucumber Sauce

MAIN INGREDIENTS

100g [4oz] fillet of Scotch salmon,
   skinned and cut into 4 cubes
100g [4oz] fillet of turbot, skinned
   and cut into 4 equal pieces
200g [8oz] lobster tail meat,
   cooked and sliced into 4
   medallions
4 scallops with coral, shelled and
   washed
4 langoustines, cooked and shelled
4 mussels, cooked and shelled
juice of $\frac{1}{2}$ lemon
salt and white pepper

SAUCE

300ml [12fl oz] warm champagne
   and cucumber sauce, *page 140*

PRESENTATION

2 tomatoes, peeled, seeded and
   quartered
12 cucumber 'barrels'
24 cucumber balls

1 Either steam or gently poach the salmon and turbot and cucumber
   'barrels' for 2 minutes. Add the other fish and cucumber balls, and
   cook for a further 2 minutes. Season with salt, pepper and lemon
   juice.

2 Arrange equal amounts of warm sauce on four warm plates. Top
   with the fish and decorate.

*Use whatever shellfish appeals to you – few households will be able to find
just four slices of lobster or four mussels.*

FILLET OF BRILL WITH LOBSTER
and a Lobster and Spinach Mousse
served on a Chervil Sauce

MAIN INGREDIENTS

4 × 75g [3oz] fillets of brill, skinned
juice of $\frac{1}{2}$ lemon
8 large spinach leaves, blanched
  and central rib removed
100g [4oz] lobster and spinach
  mousse, *page 144*
150g [6oz] raw tail meat from
  650g [1$\frac{1}{2}$lb] lobster: use claws
  and head for mousse
salt and white pepper

SAUCE

300ml [12fl oz] warm dry
  vermouth and chervil sauce,
  page 142
2 tomatoes, peeled, seeded and
  diced

PRESENTATION

4 sprigs of chervil

---

1 Season the fillets with salt, pepper and lemon juice.

---

2 Wrap each brill fillet in two blanched spinach leaves. Make a deep
   incision through the spinach and into the fish. Pipe the lobster and
   spinach mousse into the incision.

---

3 Cut the lobster tail into twelve small medallions.

---

4 Steam the brill parcels for 6 minutes. Insert three pieces of lobster
   into the half-cooked mousse in each fillet. Steam for a further
   4 minutes.

---

5 Add diced tomato to the sauce. Warm through.

---

6 Divide the sauce between four warm plates. Place a brill parcel on
   each plate. Decorate with chervil sprigs.

---

*Fillets of white fish such as brill and turbot make excellent containers for
mousses and other fillings.*

FRICASSÉE OF MONKFISH, MUSSELS AND VEGETABLES with a Tomato and Rosemary Sauce

MAIN INGREDIENTS

200g [8oz] monkfish fillet, skinned,
  cut into 1cm [½ inch] cubes
juice of ½ lemon
650g [1½lb] mussels, cooked and
  shelled: reserve juices for sauce
325g [12oz] vegetables, blanched:
  e.g. mangetouts, broccoli florets,
  asparagus tips, French beans
salt and white pepper

SAUCES

200ml [8fl oz] warm rosemary
  sauce, *page 146*
150ml [6fl oz] warm tomato and
  rosemary sauce, *page 147*

PRESENTATION

sprigs of chervil
1 tsp truffle, finely diced

---

1 Season monkfish cubes with salt, pepper and lemon juice. Steam for
   about 6 minutes.

---

2 Add the mussels, vegetables and monkfish to the rosemary sauce.
   Warm through. Season.

---

3 Pour a ring of tomato and rosemary sauce round the edge of four
   warm plates. Divide the fricassée equally and spoon it on to the
   middle of each plate. Decorate.

---

*A good dish, cheaper to make than most. You could substitute flakes of cod
or haddock for the monkfish.*

Trio of Vegetable Packets enclosing Oysters, Scallops and Langoustine with a Saffron and Ginger Sauce

MAIN INGREDIENTS

2 leeks, blanched
4 oysters, shelled
50g [2oz] unsalted butter, clarified
4 langoustine tails, cooked and
  shelled
4 scallops, shelled and washed
4 Savoy cabbage leaves, blanched
  and central rib removed
325g [12oz] hot scallop mousse,
  page 146
4 spinach leaves, blanched and
  central rib removed
salt and white pepper

SAUCE

300ml [12fl oz] warm saffron and
  ginger sauce, *page 146*, with
  finely chopped chives added

PRESENTATION

saffron stamens, soaked in warm
  water
chives, whole

1 Split the leeks in two lengthways and select eight of the larger outside leaves. Dry them and set aside. (Use the remainder for another recipe.)

2 Sauté the oysters for 20 seconds each side in warm butter. Season. Remove and drain on kitchen paper. Cook the langoustine tails and scallops for the same length of time, but at a slightly higher temperature to give them a little colour. Season and drain them.

3 Wrap each langoustine tail in a cabbage leaf together with a tablespoonful of scallop mousse. Wrap the scallops in spinach leaves, again with a tablespoonful of mousse. Place a tablespoonful of mousse in the centre of each of four of the leek leaves, and top with oysters. Cover each oyster with a second leek leaf placed at right angles to the first leaf and tucked underneath. Trim the leek leaves if too long.

4 Steam the packages for about 8 minutes, or cook for a similar time in a medium oven in a little white wine or fish stock.

5 Divide the sauce between four warm plates and place the parcels on top. Decorate with saffron and chives.

Blanched lettuce leaves would also make good parcels.

MAGRET of DUCK WITH FIGS
on a Sauce enriched with a fig Coulis

MAIN INGREDIENTS
1 duck magret (or 2 breasts of
   Aylesbury duckling)

SAUCE
2 tbsp raspberry vinegar
300ml [12fl oz] duck stock,
   page 142
200ml [8fl oz] fig coulis, *page 142*
50g [2oz] cold unsalted butter,
   diced
salt and black pepper

PRESENTATION
4 fresh figs
2 oranges, peeled and segmented

1 Place the duck skin side down in a frying pan with no fat or oil.
  Cook over a moderate heat until skin crisps and most of the natural
  fats have come out. Drain off the fat. Turn the duck over and cook
  for a further 3 minutes. The meat should be pink when cut. (The
  duck can be grilled if preferred.)

2 Remove the duck from pan and keep warm. Deglaze the pan with
  vinegar and add the duck stock. Boil to reduce by half. Add fig
  coulis and again boil to reduce until approximately 300ml [12fl oz].
  Strain the sauce and return to pan. Add the cold butter piece by
  piece. Season.

3 Put the figs into a medium oven to warm through for 5 minutes.
  Take them out and cut into six sections through the stem, but leave
  the sections attached to the base.

4 Thinly slice the duck breasts. Arrange equal amounts of sauce on
  four warm plates. Put the duck fillets on top and decorate.

Boned Quail in Pastry
filled with a Game Mousse and served with a Port and Orange Sauce

MAIN INGREDIENTS

4 quails, boned
50g [2oz] unsalted butter, clarified
4 circular croûtons, 5cm [2 inches] diameter, cut from slices of white bread
4 sheets filo pastry
200g [8oz] game mousse, *page 142*
4 grapes, peeled and seeded
salt and black pepper

SAUCE

300ml [12fl oz] warm port and orange sauce, *page 145*

PRESENTATION

1 leek, julienned and blanched, warmed in butter before serving
1 orange, peeled and segmented
8 grapes, peeled, halved and seeded

---

1 Fry the quails in 25g [1oz] butter on all sides until the skin is brown. Season. Remove from pan and cut each one in half along the length of the breast.

---

2 Fry the croûtons in the same pan until golden on both sides.

---

3 Brush both sides of each sheet of pastry with the remaining clarified butter. Fold in half.

---

4 Place a fried croûton in the middle of each sheet of pastry. Divide the game mousse equally between the croûtons, shape into a mound and top with a grape. Surround this with the quail halves. Gather the four corners of the pastry, and pinch and twist to make a parcel, as in the diagrams on *page 138*. Roast in a medium oven for 20 minutes, covering the top with foil if they become too brown. Drain the quail parcels on kitchen paper. Arrange on warm plates with the sauce and decorate.

MEDALLION OF VENISON WITH OYSTER MUSHROOMS on a Garlic Cream and a Gin and Juniper Sauce

MAIN INGREDIENTS

4 × 25g [1oz] slices fresh duck foie
    gras
25g [1oz] unsalted butter, clarified
4 × 100g [4oz] medallions of saddle
    venison, previously marinated,
    page 144
8 oyster mushrooms, washed and
    dried
100g [4oz] game mousse,
    preferably venison, *page 142*
4 thin slices truffle
24 chervil sprigs
4 squares caul fat
salt and black pepper

SAUCES

150ml [6fl oz] warm gin and
    juniper sauce, *page 143*: made
    using the marinade
150ml [6fl oz] cold garlic cream,
    page 143

PRESENTATION

1 tsp truffle, finely diced
100g [4oz] fresh duck foie gras,
    sautéed and diced

---

1 Sauté the foie gras slices for 15 seconds each side (no extra fat is
   needed). Season. Allow to cool on kitchen paper so that excess fat is
   absorbed.

---

2 Add the butter to the same pan. Fry the venison medallions on both
   sides until brown, approximately 30 seconds on each side. Season
   and remove. Add the oyster mushrooms. Sauté for 1 minute each
   side, and season.

---

3 When all these ingredients are cold, place the four venison
   medallions on a flat surface. Put a piece of foie gras on top of the
   medallion and a spoonful of mousse on the foie gras. Smooth with a
   palette knife. On top of the mousse place an oyster mushroom,
   truffle slice and chervil sprigs, and wrap the whole parcel in the
   caul fat. Cook in a medium oven for 8 to 10 minutes. For the last
   2 minutes of cooking add the remaining four oyster mushrooms to
   warm through.

---

4 Spoon the gin and juniper sauce over half of each plate and the
   garlic cream over the other half. The two sauces will remain
   separate. Place an oyster mushroom and a medallion in the middle.
   Decorate with diced truffle and foie gras.

---

*Venison is becoming more popular as the growth in deer-farming makes it
more available and less expensive.*

Saddle of Hare with Prunes and a Celeriac Mousse, served on a Horseradish and Onion Sauce

MAIN INGREDIENTS
1 saddle of hare, sinews removed
cooked marinade, *page 144*
325g [12oz] celeriac mousse,
   page 140
50g [2oz] unsalted butter, clarified
50g [2oz] cold, unsalted butter,
   diced
salt and black pepper

SAUCE
200ml [8fl oz] warm horseradish
   and onion sauce, *page 143*

PRESENTATION
12 prunes, stoned
4 tbsp brandy
4 tbsp cold tea

---

1 Twenty-four hours in advance, marinate the hare in cooked marinade. Soak the prunes in brandy and tea.

---

2 Butter the inside of four ramekins, and fill with celeriac mousse. Smooth the top and tap the dishes on a hard surface to remove any air bubbles. Place in a roasting tin half full of warm water. Cook in a medium oven for about 12 to 15 minutes. Test by inserting the tip of a knife or skewer into the mousse: if it comes out clean the mousse is cooked.

---

3 Remove the meat from the marinade, reserving the marinade. Roast the meat in a hot oven for 12 minutes, basting occasionally with the remaining clarified butter.

---

4 Simmer the prunes in their liquid for 15 minutes. Strain, and add the juice to the meat marinade. Boil to reduce by half. Season. Add the cold butter pieces, stirring until emulsified. Halve four of the prunes and dice the rest.

---

5 Remove the meat from the saddle and slice it into thin strips.

---

6 Turn the mousses out on to four plates and top with diced prunes. Arrange meat, prune halves and sauces around them.

Venison or rabbit can be used as a substitute for hare. Try with a Jerusalem artichoke mousse for a change.

Fillet of Scotch Beef with fresh Duck foie Gras and two Truffle Sauces

MAIN INGREDIENTS

25g [1oz] unsalted butter, clarified
4 × 75g [3oz] fillets of Scotch beef
4 × 25g [1oz] slices fresh duck
   foie gras
salt and black pepper

SAUCES

150ml [6fl oz] warm dark truffle
   sauce, *page 148*
150ml [6fl oz] warm white truffle
   sauce, *page 148*

PRESENTATION

2 slices truffle, julienned
1 orange, peeled and segmented
8 sprigs of chervil

---

1 Heat the butter in a pan. Sauté the fillets for approximately
  3 minutes on each side. Season. Remove from pan and keep them
  warm.

---

2 In a hot clean pan sauté the foie gras slices for 20 seconds on each
  side (no extra fat is needed). Season. Place a piece of foie gras on top
  of each fillet.

---

3 Deglaze the pan with the dark truffle sauce and stir.

---

4 Divide the sauces between four warm plates, pouring the white
  truffle sauce around the edge of the plate and the dark sauce in the
  centre. Place one fillet topped with foie gras in the middle of each
  plate and decorate.

---

*An expensive but pleasing dish. If you need a substitute for the foie gras, try
chicken liver or calf's liver.*

Calf's Sweetbreads, Liver and Kidney
served with Ogen Melon and Saffron Sauce

MAIN INGREDIENTS

4 × 40g [1½oz] slices Dutch calf's
  liver
1 small calf's sweetbread, cooked
  and cut into 4 slices
1 small calf's kidney, without suet,
  soaked in milk for 30 minutes
25g [1oz] unsalted butter, clarified
1 tbsp cooking oil
salt and white pepper

SAUCE

300ml [12fl oz] warm saffron and
  ginger sauce, *page 146*

PRESENTATION

1 small Ogen melon, scooped into
  balls with medium parisienne
  cutter
4 cherry tomatoes, peeled, seeded
  and quartered

---

1 Season the liver and sweetbread.

---

2 Remove the kidney from the milk and cut it in half lengthways.
Remove the core. Halve each piece again. Season and set aside.

---

3 Heat half the butter and the oil in frying pan. Add the kidney and
liver to the hot fat, browning both sides. Add the sweetbread and
brown. Sauté until the liver and kidney are sufficiently cooked.
Drain the meats on kitchen paper.

---

4 Sauté the melon lightly in the remaining butter.

---

5 Divide the sauce between four warm plates. Place the meats and the
melon balls on the sauce and decorate.

---

*Offal in most forms is regaining its popularity. Beautiful textures combined
with the unusual flavour of a saffron sauce make this dish memorable.*

Ballotine of Baby Chicken with Crab, Cucumber and Ginger on a Tomato and Garlic Sauce

MAIN INGREDIENTS

¼ cucumber, peeled, seeded and
  finely diced
1 tsp finely chopped fresh ginger
150ml [6fl oz] dry white wine
4 baby chicken legs, boned: see
  diagram, *page 139*
100g [4oz] hot scallop mousse,
  page 146
150g [6oz] white crab meat
4 squares caul fat
25g [1oz] unsalted butter, clarified
salt and white pepper

SAUCE

300ml [12fl oz] warm tomato and
  garlic sauce, *page 147*

PRESENTATION

½ cucumber, peeled, cut into 1cm
  [½ inch] slices, centres removed to
  make rings: reserve peel
1 tomato, peeled, seeded and finely
  chopped
cucumber peel, julienned
1 tsp chives, chopped

---

1 Earlier in the day, salt the cucumber dice and the cucumber rings. Leave for 30 minutes, then drain and rinse to remove excess salt. Blanch the cucumber rings for 3 minutes, cucumber dice and peel for 1 minute and the ginger for 1 minute in the dry white wine. Drain and set aside to cool. (Use the wine for the sauce.)

---

2 Season the inside of the chicken legs.

---

3 Mix the mousse, crab meat, cucumber dice and ginger thoroughly.

---

4 Using a teaspoon or a piping bag fill the chicken legs with crab mixture. Fold the caul fat over the legs, sealing in the crab. (See diagram on *page 139*.) Fill the cucumber rings with chopped tomato. Steam the chicken legs for approximately 12 to 15 minutes. For the last 2 minutes place the cucumber rings in the steamer to warm through. Remove the legs from the steamer, and sauté gently in butter, skin side first, until golden brown. Drain.

---

5 Divide the sauce between four warm plates. Place the chicken on the sauce. Add three cucumber rings and some julienned cucumber peel to each plate. Decorate.

FEUILLETÉ OF PARTRIDGE AND MANGO
with a Spinach Sauce and a Mango Coulis

MAIN INGREDIENTS

2 oven-ready partridges
2 rashers fat bacon
50g [2oz] unsalted butter, clarified
1 shallot, chopped
1 clove garlic, chopped
8 puff pastry crescents, cooked and
    halved horizontally
salt and black pepper

SAUCES

150ml [6fl oz] warm spinach sauce,
    page 147
150ml [6fl oz] warm mango coulis,
    page 144

PRESENTATION

1 mango, peeled and flesh julienned
tiny rolls of blanched spinach
    leaves

1 Season the partridges. Place bacon over the breasts and tie with
   string. Roast for 10 minutes in a hot oven.

2 Remove bacon, breasts and legs. Lower the temperature and return
   the breasts to the oven for 8 minutes. Skin the legs and cut off the
   meat. Chop finely.

3 Sweat the chopped shallot and garlic in butter until soft, and add
   the chopped partridge legs. Season.

4 Remove the partridge breasts from oven and put the pastry cases
   into the oven for 2 minutes to warm through. Slice the breasts
   thinly.

5 Place a spoonful of mango coulis in the centre of four warm plates
   and pour the spinach sauce round the edge of the plate. Put the
   bottom halves of the pastry crescents on top of the mango coulis
   and place a spoonful of the diced leg between the crescents. Arrange
   the strips of partridge around the edge of the pastry bottoms, put on
   the pastry lids and top with mango julienne. Decorate with sliced
   spinach rolls.

Beef and Veal 'Burgers' with Oysters and Spinach

MAIN INGREDIENTS

1 shallot, finely chopped
50g [2oz] unsalted butter, clarified
8 oysters, shelled and finely chopped: reserve sieved juices for oyster cream
2 tbsp cream mixed with 1 egg yolk
8 leaves spinach, blanched, central rib removed
200g [8oz] veal fillet trimmings, finely chopped
200g [8oz] beef fillet trimmings, finely chopped
8 squares caul fat
salt and black pepper

SAUCES

100g [4oz] bone marrow, poached and diced
150ml [6fl oz] warm red burgundy sauce, *page 146*
150ml [6fl oz] warm oyster and champagne sauce, *page 145*

PRESENTATION

1 tomato, peeled, seeded and julienned
cucumber peel, blanched and julienned
100g [4oz] bone marrow, poached and diced

---

1 Sweat the shallot in half the butter, add the chopped oysters and cook for 30 seconds over a fast heat. Season with ground black pepper. Drain any juices that may have been released by the cooking, and use these for the sauce. Add cream and egg yolk mixture to the oysters. Cook for 1 minute without boiling. Allow to cool.

---

2 Spread the spinach leaves on a flat surface, season, and place a teaspoonful of the cold oyster mixture on each leaf. Wrap up.

---

3 Divide both the veal and beef into four equal amounts. Season well. Shape each into a 'burger'; make an indentation in the centre of each in which to place an oyster parcel. Mould the meat around the parcel to cover it completely. Wrap each 'burger' in caul fat. Sauté them in the remaining butter to brown all sides, then put them in a medium oven for 5 to 8 minutes.

---

4 Add diced marrow to the burgundy sauce. Heat through.

---

5 Place two spoonfuls of oyster and champagne sauce on each of four warm plates. Spoon the burgundy sauce around this; the two sauces will remain separate. Place a veal 'burger' and a beef 'burger' on each circle of oyster and champagne sauce. Decorate.

A good way of using expensive trimmings. The dish also works well with finely chopped fish – monkfish proving to be the best.

Flowering Courgette
with a pastry case of Asparagus and buttered Chanterelles

MAIN INGREDIENTS

4 small courgettes with flowers
   attached
150g [6oz] wild mushroom
   mousse, *page 149*
4 round shortcrust pastry tartlet
   cases, cooked
4 tbsp tomato coulis, *page 148*
8 asparagus tips, blanched
150g [6oz] chanterelles, washed
   and dried
50g [2oz] unsalted butter, clarified
1 clove garlic, finely chopped
1 shallot, finely chopped
salt and black pepper

SAUCE

300ml [12fl oz] warm wild
   mushroom sauce, *page 149*

PRESENTATION

1 leek, julienned and blanched
1 tomato, peeled, seeded and
   julienned
1 tsp chives, chopped

---

1 Wash the courgette flowers carefully without soaking to remove any insects. Using a small piping bag fill the flowers with wild mushroom mousse. Fold the petals inwards to enclose the mousse. Steam for approximately 8 to 10 minutes until the mousse is cooked. Make several cuts lengthways along the courgette to within 1cm [½ inch] of the flower and fan it out. Keep warm.

---

2 Fill the four pastry tartlets with tomato coulis and top with seasoned, buttered asparagus tips. Place in a warm oven to heat through.

---

3 Sauté the chanterelles in the rest of the butter, with the garlic and the shallot. Season.

---

4 Spoon the sauce on to four warm plates. Arrange some mushrooms, a courgette and a tartlet on each plate. Decorate.

Fillet of Welsh Lamb
with an Aubergine Mousse
and a Tomato and Garlic Sauce

MAIN INGREDIENTS

3 bulbs of garlic, separated into
   cloves and peeled
175ml [10fl oz] goose fat
325g [12oz] aubergine mousse,
   page 140
fillet from best end of Welsh lamb
   (approx. 450g [1lb])
25g [1oz] unsalted butter, clarified
4 tbsp tomato concassé, *page 147*
salt and black pepper

SAUCE

300ml [12fl oz] warm tomato and
   garlic sauce, *page 147*

PRESENTATION

1 small bunch chives, whole

1 Cook the garlic cloves slowly in goose fat for about 1 hour. Allow to
cool in goose fat.

2 Butter four individual tartlet moulds and fill with aubergine
mousse. Cover with sheets of buttered paper. Cook in a bain-marie
in a medium oven for approximately 10 to 14 minutes.

3 Brown the lamb all over in clarified butter. Season. Remove the
mousses from the oven. Increase the temperature and roast the
lamb in the oven for 8 to 12 minutes. Turn the oven off, leaving the
lamb inside, and return the mousses to keep warm.

4 Heat the tomato concassé. Warm the garlic cloves in the goose fat
and drain. Cut the lamb into about twenty thin slices. Turn the
aubergine mousses out on to four warm plates and top with tomato
concassé and lamb. Spoon the sauce around the mousses. Decorate
with garlic cloves and chives.

FEUILLETÉ OF MORELS AND ASPARAGUS
with a Wild Mushroom Sauce

MAIN INGREDIENTS

8 small puff pastry crescents,
  cooked
50g [2oz] unsalted butter, clarified
100g [4oz] fresh morels,
  thoroughly washed and halved
28 asparagus tips, cooked
salt and white pepper

SAUCE

300ml [12fl oz] warm wild
  mushroom sauce, *page 149*

PRESENTATION

4 sprigs of chervil

---

1 Split the pastry crescents horizontally. Put them in a warm oven for
  3 minutes to heat through.

---

2 Heat the butter in a frying pan. When hot, add the morels. Fry for
  3 minutes, stirring occasionally.

---

3 Turn down the heat and add the asparagus tips to the frying pan.
  Cook for a further 2 minutes, turning regularly. Season. Drain off
  excess butter.

---

4 Divide the sauce between four warm plates. Put the bottoms of the
  pastry crescents in the centre. Arrange the asparagus and morels,
  and put the tops on the pastry crescents.

Fillet of Dutch Veal with Citrus Fruits on Caviar and a Champagne Sauce

MAIN INGREDIENTS

4 × 100g [4oz] veal fillet steaks,
    sinews removed
25g [1oz] unsalted butter, clarified
1 tbsp oil
salt and black pepper

SAUCE

300ml [12fl oz] warm champagne
    sauce, *page 141*
25g [1oz] caviar

PRESENTATION

cucumber peel, julienned and
    blanched
citrus fruits, peeled and segmented;
    the peel, julienned and blanched:
    choose from lemon, grapefruit,
    lime and orange

---

1 Season the veal with salt and black pepper. Put the butter in a
frying pan, add the oil and when hot cook the fillets for 2 to
3 minutes on each side. Drain on kitchen paper.

---

2 Add the caviar to the warm sauce just before serving. Divide the
sauce between four warm plates, place a veal fillet on each plate
and decorate.

---

*Do not use lumpfish roe as a substitute for the caviar – the taste would be
too strong.*

Feuilleté of Woodcock and Foie Gras on a Port and Cranberry Sauce

MAIN INGREDIENTS
2 woodcock, plucked, but not
　　drawn
2 rashers of bacon
50g [2oz] unsalted butter, clarified
1 shallot, chopped
1 clove garlic, chopped
150g [6oz] fresh foie gras, diced
1 tbsp port
4 puff pastry circles, cooked and
　　halved horizontally
salt and black pepper

SAUCE
300ml [12fl oz] warm port and
　　cranberry sauce, *page 145*

PRESENTATION
4 broccoli florets, blanched
100g [4oz] cranberries, blanched

1　Truss each woodcock with its own beak through the thighs, and
　　remove the eyes. Season. Place bacon over the breasts and tie with
　　string. Roast for 12 to 15 minutes in a hot oven with half the
　　butter, basting regularly. Remove the bacon, cut away legs and
　　breasts and heads, and keep warm. Remove the entrails from the
　　carcases with a small spoon, discarding the gizzards. Chop the
　　entrails.

2　Sauté the shallot and garlic in the remaining butter. Cook over a
　　low heat to soften, then add the diced foie gras and entrails. Raise
　　the heat and sauté quickly. Season and sprinkle with port. Drain
　　and keep warm. Loosen the juices in the pan with the sauce and stir
　　to combine.

3　Spread the bottom halves of the pastry cases with foie gras mixture.
　　Heat the pastry cases in a warm oven for 2 minutes.

4　Split the heads in two through the beak.

5　Carve the breasts. Toss the broccoli in butter to warm. Season.
　　Divide the sauce between four warm plates. Place the bottom half
　　of the pastry case on the sauce, and arrange the slices of breast
　　around the pastry base. Set the pastry lid on top. Arrange a leg and
　　half a head on the plate with a few cranberries and the broccoli.

*Woodcock is my favourite game bird, but snipe or wild duck make good
substitutes.*

FILLET OF VEAL WITH A 'SOUFFLÉ'
and a delicate Rosemary Sauce

MAIN INGREDIENTS

25g [1oz] unsalted butter, clarified
4 × 100g [4oz] medallions Dutch
  veal fillet
150g [6oz] chicken mousse,
  page 141; 2 extra egg whites
  whipped and folded in
100g [4oz] veal sweetbreads, diced
100g [4oz] duck foie gras, diced
$\frac{1}{4}$ red pepper, roasted, peeled and
  julienned
$\frac{1}{4}$ green pepper, roasted, peeled and
  julienned
1 slice truffle, julienned
4 pieces caul fat
salt and white pepper

SAUCE

300ml [12fl oz] warm rosemary
  sauce, *page 146*

PRESENTATION

1 small cucumber
8 asparagus spears, blanched
1 carrot, peeled, cut into sticks and
  blanched
2 slices truffle, julienned

1 Heat half the butter in a frying pan. Brown the veal medallions on all sides, season, remove from heat and allow to cool.

2 Add the diced veal sweetbreads and duck foie gras to the chicken mousse. Use a palette knife to smooth some mousse on top of each medallion. Decorate the top of the mousse with red and green pepper and truffle, as in the photograph. Wrap the medallions in the caul fat, completely enclosing the mousse. Place on a greased oven tray and put in a hot oven for 8 to 10 minutes.

3 Meanwhile, peel half the cucumber and, using a small parisienne cutter, shape into cucumber balls. Cut the unpeeled half into barrel shapes. Blanch the balls in boiling salted water for 1 minute, and the barrel shapes for 3 minutes.

4 Toss all the vegetables in the remaining butter. Season well.

5 Divide the sauce between four warm plates. Drain the vegetables and arrange them around the plates. Place the veal medallions in the middle, and top the cucumber 'barrels' with the julienne of truffle.

Not a soufflé in the true sense of the word.

Mousse of Scallops
with fillets of Welsh Lamb and Mangetouts on a Tomato and Basil Sauce

MAIN INGREDIENTS

75g [3oz] unsalted butter, clarified
325g [12oz] hot scallop mousse, *page 146*
1 fillet Welsh lamb, cut from best end (approx. 450g [1lb])

SAUCES

150ml [6fl oz] warm tomato and basil sauce, *page 147*
150ml [6fl oz] hollandaise sauce, *page 143*
75ml [3fl oz] fish stock, *page 142*

PRESENTATION

1 shallot, chopped
4 scallops with coral, shelled and diced
100g [4oz] mangetouts, blanched
1 tsp caster sugar
1 slice truffle, finely diced
salt and white pepper

1 Butter the inside of four ramekins, and fill with scallop mousse. Smooth the top, and tap the dishes on a hard surface to remove any air bubbles. Cover with buttered foil. Place in a bain-marie half full of warm water. Cook in a medium oven for approximately 12 to 15 minutes. Test by inserting the tip of a knife or skewer into the mousse: if it comes out clean the mousse is cooked. Remove them from the oven and keep warm. Raise the oven temperature.

2 Fry the lamb on all sides in some of the butter to seal it. Season and cook it in a hot oven for approximately 8 minutes.

3 Meanwhile, dilute the hollandaise with warm fish stock to a coating consistency.

4 Sweat the shallot in remaining butter until soft but not brown. Add the scallops and warm through. Season. Drain and keep warm. Toss mangetouts in the same pan with the sugar. Season.

5 When the lamb is cooked, cut it into sixteen slices and keep warm. Turn a mousse out on to each plate, absorbing excess liquid with kitchen paper. Spoon a little hollandaise over each one, then pour tomato and basil sauce around the edge. The sauces will remain separate. Place lamb and mangetouts around the plate. Top the mousse with diced scallop and sprinkle with diced truffle.

BREAST OF CORN-FED PIGEON
stuffed with a Mousse of Pigeon and Garlic served with a Red Burgundy Sauce

MAIN INGREDIENTS

3 bulbs of garlic, separated into
  cloves and peeled
3 tbsp goose fat
150ml [6fl oz] garlic cream,
  page 143
pigeon mousse using meat from
  pigeon legs and recipe for game
  mousse, *page 142* ($\frac{1}{2}$ quantity)
breasts from 2 corn-fed pigeons,
  boned
4 pieces caul fat
2 medium potatoes, peeled
salt and white pepper

SAUCES

150ml [6fl oz] warm champagne
  sauce, *page 141*, with 2 tbsp
  garlic cream, *page 143*, added
200ml [8fl oz] warm red burgundy
  sauce, *page 146*

PRESENTATION

1 tomato, peeled, seeded and diced
1 tsp chives, chopped

1 Boil the garlic in three changes of water for 5 minutes each time.
  Roast for 5 minutes in a medium oven with the goose fat.

2 Meanwhile, fold the garlic cream gently into the pigeon mousse.
  Make a deep cut in the side of each pigeon breast to form a pocket.
  Use a piping bag to fill the pocket with the pigeon and garlic
  mousse. Season. Wrap each breast in a piece of caul fat.

3 Wash and grate the potato. Heat four small all-metal frying pans or
  one larger one. Drain half the goose fat from the garlic, and put
  some into each pan. Place a small handful of grated potato in each
  hot frying pan, and press down with a palette knife to make a small
  potato cake. Brown on both sides, season and then put the pans in
  the oven for 10 to 12 minutes.

4 Put the pigeon breasts into the tray of garlic and roast for 8 to
  12 minutes. The pigeon and potato should be ready at more or less
  the same time.

5 Slice each pigeon breast. Place a spoonful of champagne and garlic
  sauce in the centre of four warm plates. Pour the burgundy sauce
  around the edge. Place a potato cake on top of the garlic sauce, and
  the sliced pigeon breast and garlic around the potato. Decorate.

'THE ULTIMATE'
Whole Truffle en Croûte
with a Morel Sauce

MAIN INGREDIENTS
1 shallot, chopped
1 clove garlic, finely chopped
25g [1oz] unsalted butter, clarified
100g [4oz] fresh duck foie gras,
  finely diced
100g [4oz] cooked spinach,
  finely chopped
4 slices Parma ham
4 truffles, approximately 40g [1½oz]
  each, cooked
4 sheets filo pastry, buttered on
  both sides
salt and black pepper

SAUCE
300ml [12fl oz] warm morel sauce,
  page 145

PRESENTATION
truffle slices, julienned
4 tbsp meat stock, boiled down to a
  full glaze

---

1 Sweat the shallot and garlic in the butter, add the foie gras, cook for
  30 seconds and then add chopped spinach. Mix well to absorb all
  the fats. Season with salt and black pepper. Allow to cool.

---

2 Spread out four slices of Parma ham on a flat surface. Place a
  spoonful of spinach mixture on each piece of ham, and then a
  truffle. Wrap into a bundle, and enclose this in filo pastry: see the
  diagram on *page 138*.

---

3 Bake in a medium hot oven for 10 minutes or until golden brown.

---

4 Divide the morel sauce between four warm plates. Place a cooked
  pastry parcel in the centre, and decorate with the truffle julienne
  and drops of meat glaze.

FILO PASTRY PARCELS

Diagrams by David Gifford

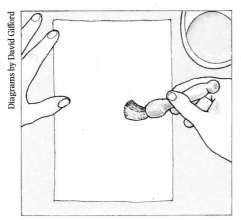

1 Brush filo on both sides with melted butter

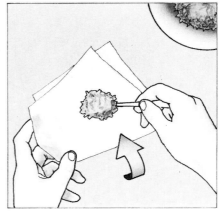

2 Fold sheet in half and place spoonful of filling in the centre.

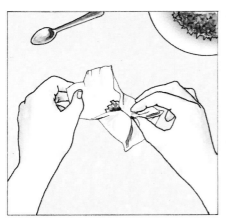

3 Bring corners together.

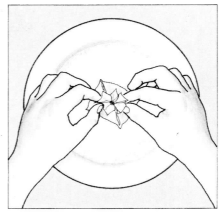

4 Pinch and twist pastry together at the top to seal the parcel. Stand on floured plate in refrigerator until ready to use.

BONING AND STUFFING A CHICKEN LEG

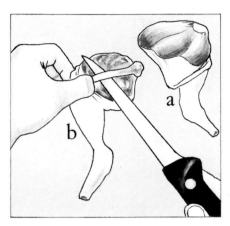

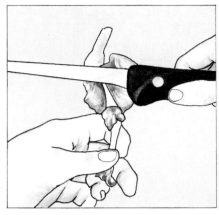

1 a Pull skin away from flesh to avoid piercing it while boning the leg.
b With leg other way up, make an incision along the flesh directly above the bone. Ease flesh off the bone; it should come away cleanly.

2 Cut around joint, then continue down second piece of bone with a scraping action. Once flesh has been cleared low enough, snap off bone at end knuckle. Trim off piece of scaly 'ankle' to leave small protrusion of bone.

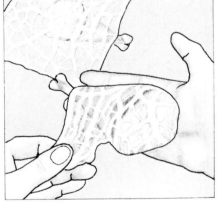

3 Pull skin back over flesh and, using piping bag, fill leg with mousse.

4 Wrap leg securely in caul fat to ensure it holds its shape.

SAUCES, MOUSSES, FILLINGS, DRESSINGS, STOCKS AND MARINADES

STOCKS Well made stocks are vital in good cooking, providing a basis for superb sauces. Make them whenever you have a little time to spare, and freeze them in small pots; or freeze in ice cube trays and turn out the cubes into labelled plastic bags. Keep pans uncovered throughout cooking. Use stock cubes only in emergencies. Meat, poultry or fish stocks can be further reduced to make a demi-glace or jelly (reduce by $\frac{1}{2}$) or a full glaze or extract (reduce by $\frac{3}{4}$); see also *page 148*. This cannot be done with vegetable stock; nor with stock cubes, which would merely become more concentrated in flavour.

SAUCES When the type of stock is not specified, use a stock based on the main ingredient of the dish which the sauce accompanies (e.g. for a chicken dish, use chicken stock in sauce, etc.). Most of the sauces can be used cold: adapt the recipe simply by leaving out the addition of cold butter at the end and by thinning the sauce, if necessary, with the stock. Unless otherwise specified, recipes make approx. 300ml [12fl oz].

AUBERGINE MOUSSE, HOT
1 shallot, finely chopped/1 clove garlic, finely chopped/25g [1oz] unsalted butter, clarified/3 medium aubergines, peeled and diced/1 sprig thyme/400ml [16fl oz] vegetable stock/4 tbsp double cream/2 whole eggs/salt and black pepper
Sweat shallot and garlic in butter. Add aubergines and thyme. Add stock. Bring to boil. Simmer till aubergines soften. Remove them. Strain stock and return to heat. Reduce to 2 tbsp. Return aubergines. Cool a little. Mix cream with eggs and add. Liquidize. Pass through fine sieve. Season. Refrigerate till needed. Cook as in recipe or in a bain-marie in a medium oven. (Makes approx. 450g [1lb].)

AVOCADO AND BASIL SORBET
2 ripe avocados, stoned and peeled/juice of 1 lemon/100g [4oz] sugar/400ml [16fl oz] water/salt/2 tbsp pesto/2 tbsp basil leaves, chopped
Purée avocados with lemon juice.

Dissolve sugar in water. Add salt, pesto and basil. Blend all ingredients in food processor till smooth. Put in ice cream machine or in tub in freezer. If in tub, stir when starting to freeze, and replace in freezer. (Makes approx. 600ml [24fl oz].)

BROCCOLI SAUCE
1 shallot, chopped/1 clove garlic, chopped/1 sprig rosemary/pinch of grated nutmeg/chopped stalks from 6 large heads broccoli/100ml [4fl oz] Alsatian wine/1 bay leaf/250ml [10fl oz] vegetable stock/florets from broccoli/125ml [5fl oz] double cream/25g [1oz] cold unsalted butter/salt and white pepper/a squeeze lemon juice
Add first 7 ingredients to stock. Bring to boil. Reduce by $\frac{1}{2}$. Strain through fine sieve. In separate pan of boiling salted water, cook broccoli florets for 7 minutes. Drain. Add to stock. Add cream. Liquidize. Reheat gently. Skim. Add butter in small pieces. Season. Add lemon juice.

CELERIAC MOUSSE, HOT
1 bulb celeriac/1 shallot, finely chopped/25g [1oz] unsalted butter, clarified/2 sage leaves/400ml [16fl oz] vegetable stock/4 tbsp double cream/1 whole egg + 2 yolks/salt and white pepper/more butter for moulds
Peel celeriac. Cut into 2cm [1 inch] cubes. Boil in plenty of water for 5 minutes. Drain. Sweat shallot in butter till soft but not coloured. Add sage, celeriac and vegetable stock. Bring to boil. Simmer for 15–18 minutes or until celeriac is tender. Drain and return liquid to heat. Boil till reduced to 2 tbsp. Return celeriac. Liquidize. Fold in cream, egg and yolks. Pass through fine sieve. Season. Butter moulds. Fill with mixture. Cover tops with buttered paper. Cook in bain-marie in medium oven for 15–20 minutes or till firm. Test by inserting skewer: if it comes out clean, mousse is cooked. (Makes approx. 325g [12oz].)

CHAMPAGNE AND BASIL SAUCE Use Champagne sauce recipe. Replace thyme with 2 tbsp pesto. Add julienned basil leaves with the cream.

CHAMPAGNE AND CUCUMBER SAUCE
$\frac{1}{2}$ cucumber, peeled, seeded and finely chopped/1 sprig rosemary/1 shallot, chopped/250ml [10fl oz] chicken stock/1 glass champagne/125ml [5fl oz] double cream/25g [1oz] cold unsalted butter/salt

and white pepper/1 tbsp champagne vinegar
Add first 3 ingredients to stock. Bring to boil. Reduce by ½. Discard rosemary. Liquidize sauce. Pass through fine sieve. Add champagne. Bring to boil. Simmer for 5 minutes. Add double cream. Simmer for 5 minutes more. Add butter a small piece at a time. Season. Add vinegar.

CHAMPAGNE SAUCE

1 sprig fresh thyme/1 shallot, chopped/ pinch of grated nutmeg/1 glass champagne/ 250ml [10fl oz] stock/250ml [10fl oz] double cream/25g [1oz] cold unsalted butter/salt and white pepper/1 tbsp champagne vinegar
Add first 4 ingredients to stock. Bring to boil. Reduce by ¾. Strain through fine sieve. Add cream. Return to heat. Simmer for 5 minutes. Add butter a small piece at a time. Season. Stir in vinegar. For a fizzy effect proceed as above, reducing stock a little further. Just before serving add: ¼ glass extra champagne.

CHICKEN GLAZE Use Chicken stock recipe and reduce by ¾.

CHICKEN MOUSSE, HOT

1 shallot, finely chopped/10g [½oz] unsalted butter, clarified/1 tbsp chicken glaze/meat from 2 large chicken breasts, skinned and boned/salt and white pepper/500ml [1 pint] double cream/2 egg whites
Sweat shallot in butter. Add chicken glaze. Leave to cool. Add rest of ingredients as in Game mousse method. Cook as in recipe or in bain-marie in a medium oven. (Makes approx. 650g [1½lb].)

CHICKEN STOCK

1 kg [2lb] chicken carcasses and giblets (except liver), chopped/1 pig's trotter or calf's foot, chopped/2 whole onions, spiked with 2 cloves each/1 carrot, thinly sliced/ 2 cloves garlic, crushed/1 stick celery, sliced/whites of 2 leeks, sliced/1 bouquet garni/½ bottle dry white wine/1 tsp white peppercorns, crushed
Put carcasses, giblets and trotter in water to cover. Bring to boil. Skim. Add all other ingredients. Add 2 litres [4 pints] water. Bring to boil. Simmer for 3–4 hours, skimming regularly and adding more water if needed. Strain through fine sieve lined with kitchen paper or wet cheesecloth. Leave to settle. Remove fat, skimming off last traces with kitchen paper. Return to heat. Reduce to 500ml [1 pint].

CHLOROPHYLL COLOURING

A paste of puréed green leaves and herbs, used to improve colour and flavour of green sauces and mousses.

1kg [2lb] spinach/1 shallot, chopped/ 1 clove garlic, chopped/fresh herbs (chervil, chives, basil, tarragon, parsley), chopped/ salt and white pepper
Put first 4 ingredients in liquidizer with 1 litre [2 pints] water and blend slowly. Pour mixture through cheesecloth into pan. Squeeze out all liquid. Discard pulp. Set over medium heat, stirring constantly. It will coagulate into a green purée on top of the water: remove from heat at once. Do not let it boil. Season. Pour slowly into cheesecloth. Let liquid run away. Scrape purée from cheesecloth. Store in closed container in refrigerator. Use sparingly.

CRAB AND ARMAGNAC SAUCE

1 shallot, finely chopped/1 clove garlic, finely chopped/25g [1oz] unsalted butter, clarified/brown meat from 1.5kg [3lb] crab, cooked/1 tsp Dijon mustard/1 sprig thyme/ 1 tsp tomato purée/2 tbsp tomato concassé (see *page 147*)/pinch of grated nutmeg/ 1 glass dry white wine/400ml [16fl oz] fish stock/125ml [5fl oz] double cream/1 tbsp port/2 tbsp armagnac/25g [1oz] more unsalted butter, cold/salt and white pepper/ a squeeze lemon
Sweat shallot and garlic in clarified butter till soft but not brown. Add crab, mustard, thyme, tomato purée, tomato concassé, nutmeg, white wine and stock. Bring to boil. Reduce by ½. Discard thyme. Liquidize mixture. Pass through fine sieve. Return to heat. Add cream, port and armagnac. Simmer for 5 minutes, stirring from time to time. Add the cold butter in pieces. Season. Add lemon juice.

CRAB AND GINGER FILLING
See Ménage à Trois fillings.

CRAB MOUSSE, COLD

1 shallot, finely chopped/25g [1oz] unsalted butter, clarified/1 tsp Dijon mustard/1 tbsp armagnac/1 tsp tomato purée/brown meat from 1.5kg [3lb] cooked crab/300ml [12fl oz] fish stock/2 leaves gelatine softened in cold water/salt and white pepper/300ml [12fl oz] double cream/3 egg whites
Sweat shallot in butter. Add mustard, armagnac and tomato purée. Add crab, then fish stock. Bring to boil. Reduce till most liquid has evaporated. Add gelatine. Liquidize and pass through a

fine sieve. Leave to cool. Season. Whip cream to soft peaks. Fold in. Beat egg whites to soft peaks. Fold in carefully. Leave to set in refrigerator. (Makes approx. 450g [1lb].)

CRANBERRY SAUCE See under Cranberries in Notes on Ingredients, *page 151.*

CREAMED EGG MOUSSE, COLD
4 eggs/4 tbsp double cream/1 shallot, finely chopped/25g [1oz] unsalted butter, clarified/1 tsp horseradish cream (*page 143*)/1 tsp chives, chopped/salt and black pepper
Break eggs neatly, reserving shells for serving. Beat with fork. Add cream. Pass through fine sieve to break down egg white. Sweat shallot in butter till soft but not brown. Add egg mixture, horseradish and chives. Cook over medium heat in non-stick pan, whisking. Season. Remove when it starts to set, cool and refrigerate. (Makes approx. 200g [8oz].)

CUCUMBER AND MINT SAUCE
Use Champagne and cucumber sauce recipe. Replace rosemary with chopped mint stalks. Replace champagne with dry white wine. Add julienned mint leaves with the cream.

DARK TRUFFLE SAUCE See Truffle sauce, dark.

DEMI-GLACE See note on stocks on *page 140.*

DILL CREAM See Dill sauce.

DILL MAYONNAISE
1 egg/juice of 2 lemons (reserve peel for decoration)/1 tsp sugar/1 tsp Dijon mustard/2 tbsp dill weed, chopped/salt and pepper/approx. 125ml [5fl oz] olive oil
Blend all ingredients except oil in liquidizer. Keep machine running. Add oil gradually till desired consistency is reached. The more oil, the thicker the mayonnaise.

DILL SAUCE OR CREAM
3 tbsp dill stalks, chopped/1 shallot, chopped/½ clove garlic, chopped/1 glass dry white wine/250ml [10fl oz] stock/250ml [10fl oz] double cream/2 tbsp dill leaves, chopped/salt and white pepper/25g [1oz] cold unsalted butter/a squeeze lemon juice
Add first 4 ingredients to stock. Bring to boil. Reduce by ¾. Strain through fine sieve. Add cream and chopped dill leaves. Simmer for 5 minutes. Add cold butter in pieces. Season. Add lemon juice. You can also add: 1 tsp Pernod or Ricard. Omit the butter if making a cold dill cream.

DRY VERMOUTH AND CHERVIL SAUCE Use Champagne sauce recipe. Replace champagne with 100ml [4fl oz] dry white vermouth. Add at start: 1 sprig rosemary/1 clove garlic, chopped. Add at end: 1 tsp each chervil and parsley, chopped.

DUCK STOCK Use Chicken stock recipe with duck carcases in place of chicken.

DUXELLE OF WILD MUSHROOMS, COLD
2 shallots, finely chopped/1 clove garlic, finely chopped/1 tbsp peanut oil/25g [1oz] unsalted butter, clarified/200g [8oz] wild mushrooms or trimmings, finely diced/salt and black pepper
Sweat shallot and garlic in oil and butter till soft. Add mushrooms. Raise heat. Cook, stirring occasionally, till mushroom juice has evaporated. Season. Refrigerate till needed. (Makes approx. 200g [8oz].)

EGG MOUSSE, CREAMED See Creamed egg mousse.

FIG COULIS
8 dried figs/3 tbsp port/3 tbsp brandy/100ml [4fl oz] water/75g [3oz] unsalted butter, clarified/salt and black pepper
Discard fig stalks. Chop figs. Soak in port and brandy for at least 45 minutes. Transfer to saucepan. Add water and 25g [1oz] butter. Cover. Simmer for 30 minutes or until most liquid has been absorbed. Purée with remaining butter. Pass through sieve. Season. Refrigerate till needed. (Makes approx. 200ml [8fl oz].)

FISH STOCK
1.5kg [3lb] bones and heads from white fish, skin and gills removed/400ml [16fl oz] dry white wine/1 stick celery/white of 2 leeks/2 tbsp mushroom trimmings/1 onion, peeled and stuck with 2 cloves/1 bouquet garni/a few parsley stalks/juice of 1 lemon/1 tsp white peppercorns, crushed
Soak bones and heads in iced salted water for 30 minutes. Break up bones. Put in saucepan with other ingredients. Cover with water. Bring to boil. Simmer for 20 minutes (no longer), skimming regularly. Strain through fine sieve lined with kitchen paper or wet cheesecloth. Return to heat and boil until reduced to 500ml [1 pint].

GAME MOUSSE, HOT
3 tbsp meat glaze/1 tbsp redcurrant jelly/1 shallot, finely chopped/1 clove garlic, finely chopped/1 sprig thyme/50g [2oz]

mushrooms, sliced/25g [1oz] unsalted butter, clarified/200g [8oz] meat from breasts of old birds (pheasant, partridge etc.)/1 tbsp brandy/1 tbsp port/pinch of grated nutmeg/1 whole egg + 2 whites/ black pepper/500ml [1 pint] double cream/ 1½ tsp salt

Heat meat glaze and redcurrant jelly till melted. Set aside. Sweat shallot, garlic, thyme and mushrooms in butter till soft but not brown. Leave to cool. Trim skin and sinews from meat. Put in food processor with shallot mixture, glaze mixture, brandy, port and nutmeg. Process till smooth. Add egg and egg whites. Pass through fine sieve into bowl set over ice. Add pepper. Add cream and salt slowly, working in with wooden spoon. Refrigerate till needed. Cook as in recipe or in a bain-marie in a medium oven. (Makes approx. 650g [1½lb].)

GAME STOCK

2kg [4lb] game carcases, venison bones etc./1 veal shin/2 whole onions, spiked with 2 cloves each/1 carrot, thinly sliced/2 cloves garlic, crushed/1 stick celery, sliced/2 leeks, sliced/1 bottle red wine/1 bouquet garni/ 1 tbsp juniper berries, roasted and crushed/ 1 blade mace/1 tsp white peppercorns, crushed/1 litre [2 pints] veal stock (golden – see recipe)

Roast bones and vegetables as in Veal stock, golden, recipe, deglazing with some of the wine. Put all ingredients in large pot with 2 litres [4 pints] water. Bring to boil. Simmer for 4 hours, skimming regularly and adding more water if needed. Strain through fine sieve lined with kitchen paper or wet cheesecloth. Leave to settle. Remove fat from top. Return to heat. Reduce to 600ml [24fl oz].

GARLIC CREAM

3 heads garlic, split into cloves, each one peeled and halved/100g [4oz] unsalted butter, clarified/1 large onion, sliced/1 bay leaf/salt and white pepper/double cream as required

Boil garlic in 3 changes of boiling water for 5 minutes each time. Drain. Put butter in saucepan. Add onion, bay leaf and garlic. Cook gently for 35 minutes, stirring occasionally. Season. Discard bay leaf. Liquidize. Pass through fine sieve. Dilute with cream to required consistency. Refrigerate till needed.

GIN AND JUNIPER SAUCE

Add to marinade once meat has been removed (*page 144*), 300ml [12fl oz] golden veal stock and 2 tbsp juniper berries, roasted and crushed. Boil until reduced by half. Stir in 50g [2oz] cold unsalted butter, a piece at a time. Just before serving add 2 tbsp gin.

GLAZE, FULL See note on stocks on *page 140.*

GOLDEN VEAL STOCK See Veal stock, golden.

HARE AND PRUNE FILLING See Ménage à Trois fillings.

HAZLENUT OIL DRESSING See Walnut oil dressing.

HOLLANDAISE SAUCE

5 tbsp white wine vinegar/4 tbsp water/ ½ tsp white peppercorns, crushed/1 bay leaf/ 4 egg yolks/200g [8oz] cold unsalted butter/salt

Boil vinegar, water, peppercorns and bay leaf until reduced to 2 tbsp. Strain into double boiler. When slightly cooled, stir in egg yolks. Keep double boiler over low heat. Add butter in small cubes, one at a time, stirring constantly to blend in each one completely before adding the next. Sauce will gradually thicken. Avoid overheating, which will curdle it. Season. Cover sauce with greaseproof paper and keep in a warm place till needed. It will only keep for a short time, and cannot be reheated. The sooner it is served, the better it tastes. (Makes approx. 200ml [8fl oz].)

HORSERADISH AND ONION SAUCE

200g [8oz] white onions, finely sliced/ 1 clove garlic, chopped/25g [1oz] unsalted butter, clarified/250ml [10 fl oz] stock/1 bay leaf/2 sage leaves/250ml [10fl oz] double cream/1 tbsp horseradish cream (*below*)/ 25g [1oz] cold unsalted butter/salt and white pepper/a dash Worcester sauce

Sweat onions and garlic in clarified butter till soft, not brown. Add stock, bay leaf and sage. Bring to boil. Reduce by ½. Discard bay leaf. Liquidize stock, cream and horseradish. Return to heat. Skim. Add cold butter in small pieces. Season with salt and pepper. Add Worcester sauce.

HORSERADISH CREAM

100ml [4oz] double cream/2 tbsp grated horseradish/3 tbsp lemon juice/¼ tsp salt/ ⅛ tsp paprika/a pinch cayenne

Beat cream till stiff. Fold in other ingredients a little at a time. Refrigerate till needed. Use within 2 days.

JELLIED STOCK See note on stocks, *page 140*, and Veal, beef, chicken or game jelly.

LEEK AND ROQUEFORT MOUSSE, COLD

450g [1lb] leeks, roughly chopped/500ml [1 pint] vegetable stock/2 shallots, finely chopped/1 clove garlic, finely chopped/ 2 leaves sage/25g [1oz] unsalted butter, clarified/4 leaves gelatine softened in cold water/100g [4oz] Roquefort/salt and black pepper/300ml [12fl oz] double cream/4 egg whites

Boil leeks in vegetable stock till tender. Meanwhile sweat shallot, garlic and sage in butter till soft. Strain leeks, reserving stock. Return stock to heat. Reduce to 150ml [6fl oz]. Add gelatine. Let cool a little. Add Roquefort and leeks to shallots. Stir till cheese has melted. Add stock. Liquidize. Pass through medium sieve. Season. Leave to cool. Whip cream to soft peaks. Fold into mixture. Beat egg whites to soft peaks. Stir in 1 tbsp; fold in the rest. Leave to set in refrigerator. (Makes approx. 650g [1½lb].)

LOBSTER AND MINTED PEA FILLING See Ménage à Trois fillings.

LOBSTER AND SPINACH MOUSSE, HOT

300g [12oz] uncooked lobster meat, including coral/150g [6oz] spinach, cooked, drained and finely chopped/2 whole eggs + 2 whites/400ml [16fl oz] double cream/1½ tsp salt

Blend lobster meat and spinach in food processor till smooth. Blend in eggs and whites. Pass through fine sieve into bowl set over ice. Work in cream and salt gradually with wooden spoon. Refrigerate till needed. Cook as in recipe or in a bain-marie in a medium oven. (Makes approx. 750g [1¾lb].)

MANGO COULIS

2 ripe mangoes, peeled, stoned and chopped/ ½ bottle champagne or sparkling wine/2 tbsp honey/juice of ½ lemon

Liquidize all ingredients. Pass through fine sieve. Instead of champagne, a mixture of vegetable stock and dry white wine can be used. Refrigerate till needed. (Makes approx. 500ml [1 pint].)

MARINADE, COOKED, FOR GAME, FISH OR POULTRY

1 carrot, thinly sliced/1 stick celery, chopped/1 onion, thinly sliced/2 cloves garlic, chopped/3 tbsp olive oil/500ml [1 pint] red or white wine/2 tbsp red or

white wine vinegar/1 tbsp coriander seeds, crushed/1 tbsp juniper berries, roasted and crushed/400ml [16fl oz] water

Use red wine and red wine vinegar for dark meats. Sweat vegetables in oil for 10 minutes. Add other ingredients. Bring to boil. Simmer for 35 minutes. Strain. This marinade can also be used uncooked, in which case do not strain and marinate meat for 2 hours longer.

MEAT GLAZE See note on stocks on *page 140*.

MEAT STOCK Use Chicken stock recipe with beef bones instead of chicken carcases.

MÉNAGE À TROIS FILLINGS
For assembly, see *page 138*.

CRAB AND GINGER (8 parcels)

1 shallot, finely chopped/1 clove garlic, finely chopped/2 tsp finely chopped ginger/ 25g [1oz] unsalted butter, clarified/white meat from 1kg [2lb] crab, cooked/ ¼ cucumber, peeled, seeded and finely diced/ 4 tbsp saffron and ginger sauce (*page 146*)/ salt and black pepper

Sweat shallot, garlic and ginger slowly in butter till soft but not brown. Add crab, cucumber and sauce. Bring to boil. Season. Cool before use.

HARE AND PRUNE (4 parcels)

4 prunes, soaked in brandy and tea/ ½ shallot, chopped/1 small clove garlic, chopped/10g [½oz] unsalted butter, clarified/ 100g [4oz] marinated hare meat, diced/ 2 tbsp soured cream/salt and cayenne pepper

Cook prunes in soaking liquid for 20 minutes. Let cool. Drain, halve and stone. Keep 4 halves, dice rest. Sweat shallot and garlic in butter till soft but not brown. Add drained meat and diced prunes. Raise heat. Cook for 2 minutes. Add sour cream. Cook for 30 seconds, stirring. Season. Cool before use. Put a prune half on pastry and top with mixture.

LOBSTER AND MINTED PEA (4 parcels)

100g [4oz] pea and mint purée (*page 145*)/ 100g [4oz] lobster meat, cooked/2 tbsp cold champagne sauce (*page 141*)

Place ingredients on pastry in above order.

PIGEON, RED CABBAGE AND APPLE (8 parcels)

50g [2oz] streaky bacon/1 tbsp goose fat/ 200g [8oz] red cabbage, without stalk, finely chopped/2 Cox's apples, peeled, cored and finely diced/2 tbsp sultanas, soaked in

brandy/1 tbsp redcurrant jelly/1 tbsp port/
3 tbsp game stock/salt and black pepper/
pinch of grated nutmeg/1 shallot, finely
chopped/2 pigeon breasts, skinned, boned
and diced/3 tbsp game glaze

Brown bacon in half goose fat. Add
cabbage, apple, sultanas and
redcurrant jelly. Stir. Add port and
stock. Cover. Cook slowly for 2 hours.
Season. Add nutmeg. Leave to cool.
Sweat shallot in rest of goose fat till soft.
Add pigeon. Raise heat and sauté for
2 minutes. Add meat glaze. Cook for
30 seconds. Season. Put spoonful of
cabbage mixture on pastry. Top with
spoonful of pigeon.

TURBOT AND LEEK (4 parcels)
4 × 2cm [1 inch] cubes turbot/salt and white
pepper/a squeeze lemon/4 tbsp leek julienne
softened in butter

Season fish; sprinkle with lemon juice.
Steam for 1 minute. Let cool. Put a
spoonful of leek mixture on pastry. Top
with turbot.

VENISON AND CRANBERRY
(4 parcels)
½ shallot, finely chopped/½ tsp finely chopped
garlic/10g [½oz] unsalted butter, clarified/
100g [4oz] venison, finely diced/2 tbsp
cranberry sauce/1 tbsp game glaze/1 tbsp
brandy/salt and black pepper

Sweat shallot and garlic in butter till
soft. Add venison. Raise heat and cook
for 2 minutes. Add cranberry sauce,
game glaze and brandy. Season. Let
cool before use.

MINTED ORANGE SAUCE
juice of 3 oranges/juice of ½ lemon/1 shallot,
chopped/1 bay leaf/2 tbsp mint stalks,
chopped/250ml [10fl oz] stock/250ml
[10fl oz] double cream/25g [1oz] cold
unsalted butter/1 tbsp mint leaves,
julienned/salt and white pepper/1 tbsp mint
vinegar

Add first 5 ingredients to stock. Bring to
boil. Reduce by ⅔. Strain. Add cream.
Simmer for 5 minutes. Add butter in
small pieces. Add mint. Season. Add
vinegar.

MOREL MOUSSE OR SAUCE
Use Wild mushroom mousse or sauce
recipe. Omit garlic in the mushroom
sauce recipe. Use morels whenever
other mushrooms are mentioned.
Reserve a few rings of cooked morel to
garnish.

MUSHROOM MOUSSE OR
SAUCE See Wild mushroom mousse
or sauce recipe.

NETTLE AND SORREL SAUCE
2 tbsp chopped shallot/1 clove garlic,
chopped/1 sage leaf/25g [1oz] unsalted
butter, clarified/100g [4oz] young sorrel
leaves/100g [4oz] young nettle leaves/
400ml [16fl oz] stock/1 bay leaf/100ml
[4fl oz] dry white wine/250ml [10fl oz]
double cream/25g [1oz] cold unsalted
butter/salt and black pepper

Sweat shallot, garlic and sage in
clarified butter till soft. Add sorrel and
nettles. Allow their juices to sweat out.
Add stock, bay leaf and wine. Bring to
boil. Reduce by ½. Liquidize. Pass
through fine sieve. Add cream. Simmer
for 5 minutes. Add cold butter in small
pieces. Season.

OYSTER AND CHAMPAGNE
SAUCE
Use Champagne sauce recipe, adding
strained juice from 12 oysters at the
start. Finish as usual, adding if you like:
diced oysters.

PEA AND MINT PURÉE
1 clove garlic, finely chopped/3 spring
onions, finely sliced/25g [1oz] unsalted
butter, clarified/200g [8oz] peas, shelled/
1 lettuce, shredded/1 tsp sugar/300ml
[12fl oz] vegetable stock/2 tbsp mint leaves,
finely chopped/2 tbsp double cream/salt and
black pepper

Sweat garlic and spring onions in
butter till soft. Add peas, lettuce, sugar
and stock. Cook till peas are tender.
Strain and return liquid to pan. Bring to
boil. Add mint. Reduce to 2 tbsp. Add
cream and peas. Liquidize. Season.
(Makes approx. 300ml [12fl oz].)

PESTO See under Basil in Notes on
Ingredients, page 150.

PIGEON, RED CABBAGE AND
APPLE FILLING See Ménage à Trois
fillings.

PORT AND CRANBERRY
SAUCE
Use Port and orange sauce recipe, but
with juice of only 1 orange. Replace
the redcurrant jelly with cranberry
sauce.

PORT AND ORANGE SAUCE
125ml [5fl oz] veal stock, golden/125ml
[5fl oz] dry red wine/ juice of 3 oranges/juice
of ½ lemon/2 tbsp redcurrant jelly/1 shallot,
chopped/1 clove garlic, chopped/½ tsp
chopped ginger/1 sprig thyme/1 bay leaf/
4 tbsp ruby port/60g [2½oz] cold unsalted
butter/1 tbsp raspberry vinegar

Put first 10 ingredients in a pan. Bring
to boil. Reduce by ¾, skimming

regularly. Strain. Add port. Simmer 5 minutes. Add butter in small pieces. Season. Add vinegar.

PUMPKIN SAUCE

200g [8oz] pumpkin, peeled and finely diced/1 shallot, chopped/1 clove garlic, chopped/1 sage leaf/pinch of grated nutmeg/1 tsp tomato purée/1 tsp sugar/ 500ml [1 pint] stock/50g [2oz] Emmenthal, grated/250ml [10fl oz] double cream/25g [1oz] cold unsalted butter/salt and white pepper/a squeeze lemon juice

Add first 7 ingredients to stock. Bring to boil. Cook till pumpkin is soft. Add Emmenthal. Simmer till melted. Discard sage. Liquidize. Pass through fine sieve. Add cream. Simmer for 5 minutes, adding extra stock if too thick. Add butter in small pieces. Season. Add lemon juice. Made slightly thinner, this is an excellent soup.

RAVIOLI FILLING

75g [3oz] duck foie gras/salt and black pepper/1 small truffle, cooked, peeled and finely chopped/50g [2oz] wild mushroom duxelle (page 142)/2 tbsp double cream

Sauté foie gras in hot pan, without added fat, for 20 seconds each side. Let cool. Season. Dice finely. Mix with truffle, duxelle and cream. Refrigerate till needed.

RED BURGUNDY SAUCE

2 shallots, chopped/1 clove garlic, chopped/ 25g [1oz] unsalted butter, clarified/10g [½oz] flour/400ml [16fl oz] stock/250ml [10fl oz] red burgundy/1 bay leaf/1 sprig thyme/1 tsp sugar/3 tbsp mushroom trimmings/25g [1oz] cold unsalted butter/salt and black pepper

Sweat shallot and garlic in clarified butter till soft and golden. Sprinkle with flour. Mix well. Add stock, wine, bay leaf, thyme, sugar and mushroom trimmings. Bring to boil. Reduce by ⅔. Strain. Add cold butter in small pieces. Season. You can also add at end: poached, diced bone marrow.

ROQUEFORT CREAM

100ml [4fl oz] still cider/white of 2 medium leeks/1 clove garlic, chopped/2 sage leaves/ 400ml [16fl oz] stock/100g [4oz] Roquefort/ 250ml [10fl oz] double cream/salt and white pepper/a squeeze of lemon juice

Add first 4 ingredients to stock. Bring to boil. Reduce by ½. Add Roquefort. Simmer gently till melted. Add cream. Liquidize. Strain through fine sieve. Season. Add lemon juice. Thin if necessary with extra stock.

ROSEMARY SAUCE Use Champagne sauce recipe. Replace champagne with dry white vermouth. Replace thyme with 6 sprigs of rosemary.

SAFFRON AND GINGER SAUCE

1 shallot, chopped/1 clove garlic, chopped/ 1 sprig thyme/2 tsp chopped fresh ginger/ 100ml [4fl oz] dry white wine/pinch of grated nutmeg/250ml [10fl oz] stock/ 250ml [10fl oz] double cream/1 tsp more finely chopped fresh ginger/½ tsp saffron, soaked in 1 tbsp warm stock/25g [1oz] cold unsalted butter/salt and white pepper/a squeeze lemon juice

Add first 6 ingredients to stock. Bring to boil. Reduce by ⅔. Strain through fine sieve. Add cream, ginger and saffron. Simmer for 5 minutes. Add butter in small pieces. Whisk. Season. Add lemon juice.

SCALLOP MOUSSE, COLD

200g [8oz] scallops (weight without shells)/ 4 tbsp dry white vermouth/½ shallot, chopped/25g [1oz] unsalted butter, clarified/ 300ml [12fl oz] fish stock/1 sprig thyme/ 2 leaves gelatine, softened in cold water/salt and white pepper/300ml [12fl oz] double cream/3 egg whites

Slice scallops thinly. Cook in vermouth for 20 seconds. Drain. Sweat shallot in butter till soft but not brown. Add the vermouth, fish stock and thyme. Reduce to 100ml [4fl oz]. Remove thyme. Add gelatine and scallops. Liquidize. Pass through fine sieve. Season. Whip cream to soft peaks. Fold into mixture. Whip egg whites to soft peaks. Fold in carefully. Leave to set in refrigerator. (Makes approx. 450g [1lb].)

SCALLOP MOUSSE, HOT

200g [8oz] scallops (weight without shells)/ 2 tbsp dry white vermouth/1 whole egg + 1 white/300ml [12fl oz] double cream/1 tsp salt/white pepper

Put scallops and vermouth in food processor. Blend. Add egg and white. Blend for 1 minute. Pass through fine sieve into bowl over ice. Work cream and salt gradually into mixture with wooden spoon. Add pepper. Refrigerate till needed. Cook as in recipe or in a bain-marie in a medium oven. (Makes approx. 450g [1lb].)

SESAME OIL DRESSING

3 spring onions, chopped/50g [2oz] ginger, chopped/4 cloves garlic, chopped/3 tbsp sesame oil/1 tbsp honey/1 tbsp soy sauce/

½ tsp five spice powder/1 tbsp coriander leaves, chopped/300ml [12fl oz] chicken stock/salt and black pepper
Sweat spring onions, ginger and garlic in sesame oil till soft but not brown. Add honey, soy sauce, five spice powder, coriander and chicken stock. Simmer for 15 minutes. Season. Leave to cool. Strain.

SMOKED COD'S ROE SAUCE, COLD
200g [8oz] smoked cod's roe/1 shallot, finely chopped/2 cloves garlic, finely chopped/1 tbsp olive oil/juice of 1 lemon/ 1 tsp tomato purée/1 tbsp chives, chopped/a dash Worcester sauce/a dash Tabasco/black pepper/300ml [12fl oz] double cream
Cut roe in half. Scrape out inside with teaspoon. Discard skin. Sweat shallot and garlic in oil. Leave to cool. Blend roe, shallot, garlic, lemon juice and tomato purée in food processor till smooth. Add chives, Worcester sauce, Tabasco and pepper. Transfer to a bowl. Stir in cream. If stiff texture preferred, first whip cream. Refrigerate till needed. (Makes approx. 500ml [1 pint].)

SMOKED SALMON MOUSSE, COLD
½ shallot, finely chopped/½ clove garlic, finely chopped/10g [½oz] unsalted butter, clarified/ 1 tsp tomato purée/300ml [12fl oz] fish stock/2 leaves gelatine, softened in cold water/150g [6oz] smoked salmon pieces/a pinch cayenne pepper/juice of ½ lemon/ 300ml [12fl oz] double cream/3 egg whites
Sweat shallot and garlic in butter. Add tomato purée and fish stock. Boil until reduced to 2 tbsp. Add gelatine and smoked salmon. Liquidize. Pass through fine sieve. Add cayenne and lemon juice. Whip cream to soft peaks. Fold into salmon purée. Whip whites to soft peaks. Fold in carefully. Leave to set in refrigerator. (Makes approx. 450g [1lb].)

SOUR CREAM DRESSING
300ml [12fl oz] soured cream/2 tbsp spring onion, finely chopped/1 tsp Worcester sauce/2 small gherkins, finely chopped/juice of ½ lemon/salt and cayenne pepper
Mix all ingredients together, seasoning to taste.

SPINACH AND DILL MOUSSE, HOT Use Spinach mousse recipe. Add, with the shallot and garlic: a handful dill weed, chopped.

SPINACH CREAM See Spinach sauce.

SPINACH MOUSSE, HOT
650g [1½lb] spinach/150ml [6fl oz] vegetable stock/2 shallots, chopped/1 clove garlic, chopped/50g [2oz] unsalted butter, clarified/salt and black pepper/1 whole egg + 2 yolks/4 tbsp double cream/1 tsp chlorophyll colouring (page 141)/more butter for moulds
Cook spinach quickly in vegetable stock till tender. Drain, reserving stock. When cool, squeeze out liquid. Boil liquid and reserved stock till reduced to 2 tbsp. Sweat shallot and garlic in butter till soft but not brown. Add spinach and stock. Season. Liquidize. Add egg, yolks, cream and chlorophyll colouring. Pass through fine sieve. Cook as in recipe or as for Celeriac mousse. (Makes approx. 325g [12oz].)

SPINACH SAUCE OR CREAM
Use Nettle and sorrel sauce recipe. Replace sorrel and nettle with equal amount of spinach. After adding cream, add ½ tsp chlorophyll colouring (page 141). Omit addition of cold butter for a cold spinach cream.

STOCKS See note on stocks (page 140), Chicken stock, Fish stock, Game stock, Veal stock, golden, and Vegetable stock.

TOMATO AND BASIL SAUCE
2 tsp chopped shallot/100ml [4fl oz] dry white wine/4 tomatoes, peeled, seeded and chopped/2 tbsp pesto/1 tsp tomato purée/ 250ml [10fl oz] stock/250ml [10fl oz] double cream/25g [1oz] cold unsalted butter/salt and white pepper/1 tbsp basil leaves, julienned/1 tbsp champagne vinegar
Add first 5 ingredients to stock. Bring to boil. Reduce by ½. Liquidize. Pass through fine strainer. Add cream. Simmer for 5 minutes. Add butter in small pieces. Season. Add basil and vinegar.

TOMATO AND GARLIC SAUCE
Use Tomato and basil sauce recipe. Omit pesto and basil. Add 3 tbsp garlic cream with the double cream.

TOMATO AND ROSEMARY SAUCE Use Tomato and basil sauce recipe. Omit pesto and basil. Add 4 sprigs rosemary at start; remove before liquidizing.

TOMATO CONCASSÉ (PULP), COOKED
2 shallots, finely chopped/2 cloves garlic, finely chopped/2 sprigs thyme/25g [1oz] unsalted butter, clarified/450g [1lb] tomatoes, peeled, seeded and diced/

1 tsp sugar/salt and white pepper
Sweat shallot, garlic and thyme in
butter till soft but not brown. Add
tomatoes and sugar. Cook over medium
heat for 15 minutes. Remove thyme.
Season. (Makes approx. 325g [12oz].)

TOMATO COULIS, UNCOOKED

*This beautiful light pink dressing is quite
different from a cooked tomato sauce.*
2 shallots, finely chopped/1 clove garlic,
finely chopped/300ml [12fl oz] olive oil/
450g [1lb] tomatoes, peeled, seeded and
chopped/1 tsp Dijon mustard/1 whole egg/
3 tbsp cider and honey vinegar/salt and
white pepper/1 tsp herbs as liked, chopped
Sweat shallot and garlic in 1 tbsp oil till
soft but not brown. Leave to cool. Put in
food processor with tomatoes, mustard,
egg and vinegar. Blend till smooth.
With blender running, add oil slowly to
form emulsion. Pass through fine sieve.
Season and add herbs. Makes approx.
500ml [1 pint].)

TRUFFLE SAUCE, DARK

400ml [16fl oz] golden veal stock/3 tbsp
truffle juice/1 tsp mushroom ketchup/3 tbsp
mushroom trimmings (wild if possible)/
1 shallot, chopped/pinch of grated nutmeg/
2 extra tbsp truffle juice/1 tbsp port/2 tsp
armagnac/60g [2½oz] cold unsalted butter/
1 tsp truffle or truffle peeling, diced/salt and
black pepper
Boil together first 6 ingredients. Reduce
by ½. Strain. Add extra truffle juice, port
and armagnac. Simmer for 3 minutes.
Skim. Add butter in small pieces.
Season. Add diced truffle.

TRUFFLE SAUCE, WHITE

1 shallot, chopped/2 tsp mushroom
trimmings, preferably wild/1 bay leaf/3 tbsp
truffle juice/1 tsp mushroom ketchup/
250ml [10fl oz] vegetable stock/250ml
[10fl oz] double cream/3 more tbsp truffle
juice/2 tsp armagnac/4 tsp port/25g [1oz]
cold unsalted butter/salt and white pepper/
1 tbsp champagne vinegar
Add first 5 ingredients to stock. Bring to
boil. Reduce by ⅔. Strain. Add cream,
extra truffle juice, armagnac and port.
Simmer for 5 minutes. Add butter in
small pieces. Season. Add vinegar. You
can also add at end: 1 tbsp white truffle
peelings, chopped.

TURBOT AND LEEK FILLING See
Ménage à Trois fillings.

VEAL, BEEF, CHICKEN OR
GAME JELLY

1.5kg [3lb] veal or beef bones or chicken or
game carcasses, chopped/2 calf's feet,
chopped/1 onion, chopped/1 bouquet garni/
200g [8oz] veal shin meat or chicken or
game scraps, finely chopped/1 more onion,
finely chopped/1 leek, finely chopped/
1 carrot, sliced/2 egg whites
Put bones or carcasses with feet, 1 onion
and bouquet garni in large pot. Cover
with water. Bring to boil. Simmer for as
long as possible (at least 6 hours),
keeping covered with water and
skimming regularly. Strain through
fine sieve lined with wet kitchen paper
or cheesecloth. Mix chopped meat and
vegetables with egg whites. Add to
stock. Bring to boil very slowly, stirring
constantly. Once simmering, leave for
30 minutes without stirring. Strain
through lined sieve. Liquid will be clear.
Leave to cool. (Makes approx. 500ml [1
pint].)

VEAL STOCK, GOLDEN

1.5kg [3lb] veal marrow bones, broken/
2 carrots, sliced/2 onions, sliced/100g [4oz]
mushroom trimmings/1 small stick celery,
sliced/½ bottle dry white wine/1 bouquet
garni/1 clove garlic, crushed/3 tomatoes,
peeled and seeded/1 tbsp tomato purée
Brown bones in hot oven, turning
regularly. After 20 minutes add carrots,
onions, mushroom trimmings and
celery. Cook for 10 minutes more.
Transfer all to large saucepan. Deglaze
roasting tray with white wine. Pour
into pan. Add bouquet garni and garlic.
Add 2 litres [4 pints] water. Bring to
boil. Simmer, skimming regularly, for
4 hours, adding tomatoes and purée
after 2 hours. There should be about
750ml [1½ pints] liquid left. Pass
through fine sieve lined with kitchen
paper or wet cheesecloth. Cool and
carefully remove fat. White veal stock is
made in the same way, but without
browning the bones.

VEGETABLE STOCK

400ml [16fl oz] dry white wine/4 tomatoes,
peeled and seeded/2 leeks, washed and
sliced/1 carrot, peeled and sliced/1 stick
celery, sliced/1 onion, peeled and spiked
with 2 cloves/4 cloves garlic, sliced/
1 bouquet garni/1 tsp white peppercorns,
crushed/1 tbsp mushroom peelings
Place all ingredients in a large
saucepan. Cover with water and bring
to the boil. Simmer for 2½ hours
skimming regularly. Pass through a
fine sieve lined with kitchen paper or
wet cheesecloth. (Makes approx. 500ml
[1 pint].)

NOTES ON INGREDIENTS

VENISON AND CRANBERRY
FILLING See Ménage à Trois fillings.

WALNUT OIL DRESSING
100ml [4fl oz] walnut oil/100ml [4fl oz] peanut oil/½ tsp Dijon mustard/1 shallot, finely chopped/1 clove garlic, finely chopped/juice of 1 lemon/3 tbsp champagne vinegar/1 bay leaf/1 sprig tarragon/salt and black pepper/½ tsp sugar
Blend all ingredients with hand whisk. Leave to settle for up to 24 hours. Pass through fine sieve. Whisk before using. A hazelnut oil dressing can be made in the same way, using hazelnut oil instead of walnut.

WATERCRESS CREAM
Use Broccoli sauce recipe. Omit rosemary. Replace broccoli with watercress, using stalks as with broccoli. Blanch leaves for 30 seconds before adding with cream. Continue as in recipe, omitting cold butter at the end.

WHITE TRUFFLE SAUCE See Truffle sauce, white.

WILD MUSHROOM DUXELLE See Duxelle of wild mushrooms.

WILD MUSHROOM MOUSSE, HOT
100g [4oz] duxelle of wild mushrooms (page 142)/150ml [6fl oz] vegetable stock/salt and black pepper/2 whole eggs + 2 whites/2 tbsp double cream
Simmer duxelle in stock till most liquid is reduced. Liquidize. Season. Mix eggs and whites with cream and add to mixture. Refrigerate till needed. Cook as in recipe or in a bain-marie in a medium oven. (Makes approx. 150g [6oz].)

WILD MUSHROOM SAUCE
4 tbsp wild mushroom trimmings/1 shallot, chopped/1 clove garlic, chopped/100ml [4fl oz] dry white wine/pinch of grated nutmeg/250ml [10fl oz] vegetable stock/ 1 more shallot, chopped/1 more clove garlic, chopped/25g [1oz] unsalted butter, clarified/ 100g [4oz] wild mushrooms, sliced/250ml [10fl oz] double cream/3 tbsp truffle juice/ 25g [1oz] cold unsalted butter/salt and black pepper
Add first 5 ingredients to stock. Bring to boil. Reduce by ½. Strain. In separate pan sweat extra shallot, garlic and wild mushrooms in clarified butter. When soft add stock and cream. Simmer for 3 minutes. Liquidize. Strain through fine sieve. Add truffle juice. Add cold butter in small pieces. Season.

NOTES ON INGREDIENTS

Many, if not most, of the recipes in this book call for luxurious ingredients or delicacies that may be hard to find or prohibitively expensive. The following list comments on many ingredients and where possible suggests alternatives. If there is no substitute, you may well be able to adapt the recipe to other ingredients. As mentioned before, the aim of this book is to fire the reader's imagination and to encourage experimentation. The only absolute requirements are that ingredients should be fresh and of prime quality so that your careful preparation and attention to detail will be repaid with first class results.

AQUAVIT Spirit flavoured with caraway. Substitute: other caraway spirits, such as kümmel, but these are sweet. If this is undesirable, steep crushed caraway seeds in vodka.

ARTICHOKES, CHINESE French: *crosnes*. Small spiral tuber good eaten raw. Wash well; no need to peel. Substitute: small turnips.

ARTICHOKES, GLOBE French: *artichauts*. Large green thistle flowers. Soak in cold salted water to remove insects. To serve whole: cook in boiling water for about 25 minutes. ARTICHOKE BOTTOMS: trim away all leaves and hairy 'choke' in middle; cook in a blanc for 10–12 minutes. Available cooked in cans (French: *fonds d'artichauts*).

ARTICHOKES, JERUSALEM French: *topinambours*. Knobbly roots. Use in mousses and purées, cooked in a blanc till tender; or cook as potatoes. Peel, if desired, after cooking.

ASPARAGUS Wild asparagus has most flavour but difficult to obtain; next best is thin English asparagus (sprue). If using tips separately, save stalks for sauces and soups. Blanch tips for 2 minutes; stalks for 4–5 minutes.

AVOCADOS Hass avocados (with knobbly, blackish skin) have most flavour. Flesh discolours once cut: avoid with a squeeze of lemon juice.

BACON For lardons buy streaky bacon in one piece. Blanch in unsalted water for 20 minutes. Cool. Cut into 5mm [¼ inch] cubes. Fry.

BASIL Herb with smooth oval leaves; easy to grow indoors. Avoid dried basil.

Preserve leaves by freezing with water in ice cubes, 3 or 4 to a cube.

BASIL BUTTER: butter flavoured with finely chopped basil leaves. Added to dishes, the butter melts, distributing the flavour throughout. Can be done with most other herbs.

BASIL SAUCE (Italian: *pesto*): good for adding to sauces and salad dressing. 200g [8oz] basil leaves/6 cloves garlic/ 200g [8oz] Parmesan/50g [2oz] pine nuts/olive oil. Blend dry ingredients in liquidizer or food processor. Add oil to make a smooth purée.

BEANS, FRENCH Choose smallest beans. Good in crudités, but blanch for 2 minutes first; 5 minutes for other uses.

BEEF Choose Scotch if possible. Finest cut is fillet; should have good marbling of fat. Trim away gristle. Remove 'chain' (gristly strip of meat) from side; save for casseroles, or mince.

BONE MARROW Butchers will generally chop up bones to make the marrow accessible. Use a spoon to scoop it out.

BROCCOLI Can be green, purple or yellow. Divide tips into clusters for decoration. Use stalks in purées, mousses and terrines. Blanch tips for 4 minutes, stalks for 8–10 minutes. Substitute: cauliflower.

CABBAGE, SAVOY Crisp, green, wrinkled leaves good as wrappings for various fillings. Discard tough outer leaves. Detach other leaves. Blanch for 3 minutes. Pare off central rib. Fill. Substitutes: other cabbages, spinach, lettuce.

CARROTS Small 'finger' carrots have more delicate flavour. Don't peel, just brush gently under running tap. Top and tail; or for certain dishes retain top with 5cm [2 inches] green stalk. Blanch whole carrots for 8–10 minutes.

CARROT BALLS: use smallest parisienne cutter, blanch for 4 minutes. JULIENNE: blanch 1–2 minutes.

CAUL FAT French: *crépine*. Fatty covering of pig's intestines. Paper thin, translucent, with network of thicker strips. Use as wrapping for meats: fat melts and bastes the meat. No real substitute; but thinly sliced streaky bacon could be used.

CAULIFLOWER Wash well in cold salted water to remove insects. Cut into small florets for decoration. Blanch for

2–4 minutes, according to size. Substitute: broccoli.

CAVIAR Sevruga is best for hot dishes, Beluga for cold. Substitutes (not nearly as good but much less expensive): 'golden caviar' and salmon eggs, from delicatessens; or, for decoration only, lumpfish roe which looks right but tastes very different from caviar, widely available.

CELERIAC Large root of a variety of celery. Nutty celery flavour. Grate raw for salads. Discolours when cut: avoid with lemon juice, or put in acidulated water. For purée: peel, slice and boil till tender.

CHAMPAGNE In sauces, substitute: dry sparkling wine.

CHANTERELLES See Mushrooms, wild.

CHERVIL Herb like delicate parsley; slight aniseed flavour. Not widely sold but easy to grow outdoors. Goes limp soon after cutting: revive by rinsing and shaking dry. Keeps for 2–3 days in salad box of refrigerator. Freeze as basil. Substitutes: parsley, fennel tops.

CHICKEN, BABY Normally known by French name: *poussin*. Choose fresh if possible; frozen have little taste. Save carcase for stock.

CHICKEN, SMOKED From delicatessens. Substitutes: smoked turkey or smoked ham.

CHICORY French: *endive*. Bleached shoots of a type of endive. Slightly bitter, becoming more so when in contact with daylight. Good in salads. Discolours easily: keep wrapped in paper before use, wash, cut or tear up and serve quickly before it goes brown.

CHIVES Small relative of onion. Stems have delicate oniony flavour, used as herb. Cut with scissors to avoid bruising. Purple flowers edible, make good decorations. Freeze as basil. Substitute: chopped spring onion tops.

CORAL See Scallops.

CORIANDER Fresh leaves resemble flat parsley but have powerful flavour: use sparingly. Sold by Middle Eastern shops, but easy to grow in sheltered spot. Freeze as basil. Substitute: parsley (but not coriander seed, which is a spice with quite different taste and uses).

CORN SALAD Also called lamb's lettuce. French: *mâche*. Small, oval salad leaves. Rather sharp flavour. Wash well to remove sand.

COURGETTES French name for
young marrows. Italian: *zucchini*.
Choose the smallest you can find.
Blanch for 3–6 minutes according to
size. Difficult to get small ones with
flowers attached unless you grow them
yourself. For recipes using flowers,
substitute: spinach or lettuce leaves
to enclose mousse.

CRABS Choose large, live Cornish
crabs. Cook for 15 minutes, or more if
very large, in boiling bouillon with
10–15g salt per litre [$\frac{1}{4}$oz per pint]. Let
cool in liquid. Discard liquid, too salty
for other use. Lever open shell. Discard
'dead man's fingers', separate brown
and white meat, pick out any shell
splinters.

CRANBERRIES Red berries with
astringent flavour. Used as decoration
or made into sauce: almost cover with
mixture of orange juice and water.
Bring to boil. Cook till berries start to
pop. Add half their weight of sugar, a
touch of nutmeg and a few cloves.
Keeps well in jars.

CROÛTONS Small circles or cubes of
stale white bread without crusts, fried
in oil till crisp and golden.

CUCUMBERS Keep in salad box of
refrigerator. Salt slices to draw out
juices which can make dishes watery.
Wipe off salt after 30 minutes. Some
people dislike the 'core' of immature
seeds, which can be removed.
CUCUMBER BALLS: peel, form with
parisienne cutter, blanch for 2 minutes.
CUCUMBER BARRELS: do not peel; cut
into short lengths, remove 'core', trim
into shapes like 'barrels', blanch for
3 minutes. Substitute: courgettes.

DANDELION LEAVES French:
pissenlits. Slightly bitter taste, less so if
very young or artificially bleached by
being grown in cellars. Bleached leaves
sold in a few greengrocers. Pick wild
leaves in spring only. Or grow your
own outdoors and bleach them by
putting a pot upside down over the
plants. Substitute: curly endive.

DILL Feathery herb with aniseed
flavour. Use seeds and leaves. Good
with salmon and in salads; leaves used
for decoration. Freeze as basil.
Substitute: fennel tops.

DUCK MAGRET Breast of specially
fattened ducks, available from
delicatessens in vacuum packets.
Firmer, meatier and tastier than
English duck breast; heavy layer of fat
under skin. Grill or fry with fat towards
heat for 4 times as long as other side, to
melt fat and crisp skin. Substitutes: see
next entry.

DUCKLING, AYLESBURY
Conventional name for common
English type. Choose fresh if possible.
Use breast as substitute for magret, legs
for mousse.

EGGS Use at room temperature for
best results. See also Quail's eggs.

ENDIVE Several types, including
chicory and radicchio (listed separately).
All slightly bitter, good in salads. Curly
endive (French: *chicorée frisée*) has
frizzy leaves, pale green with darker
edges, crisp.
BATAVIAN ENDIVE: broader leaves
like cos lettuce, sometimes with red
tinged tips. Crisper than lettuce but
more bitter.

FIGS Green, black or purple. No
special preparation, just wash.
Substitutes: not canned or dried figs,
which are quite different; use some
other exotic fresh fruit.

FILO PASTRY See Pastry.

FIVE SPICE POWDER Mixed spice
available from Chinese food stores,
consisting of aniseed, fennel seed,
cloves, cinnamon and pepper.
Substitute: individual spices.

FOIE GRAS Use duck foie gras,
cheaper than goose foie gras (though
still very expensive) and with more
flavour, in spite of being fattier. Not
widely available, except in unsuitable
pâté form. One liver weighs about 450g
[1lb]. Soak in iced water to remove
blood before cooking. Use a small knife
to scrape away any traces of gall
bladder (green patches) and cut out any
veins. Excellent served hot. Substitutes:
no real ones, but chicken livers or calf's
liver can be prepared in same way.

GARLIC Peel cloves before use. Cut
away any green centre, which can be
bitter and indigestible.

GELATINE If leaf gelatine is not
available use powdered gelatine. Refer
to packet for equivalent measures and
instructions on use. 4 leaves = approx. $\frac{1}{2}$oz
powdered gelatine.

GINGER Use fresh if possible. Peel and
chop, slice or crush to develop its
pungency. Substitutes: pickled ginger
(from Chinese shops), dried root or
ground ginger.

GOOSE FAT Very rich flavour. From specialist food stores. Substitutes: dripping or chicken fat.

GRAPEFRUIT White or pink. Peel and remove white pith. Cut between membranes to make skinless segments for garnish. Substitute: other citrus fruits.

GRAPES I like the French Muscat, beautifully sweet. To prepare: blanch in boiling water for 20 seconds, plunge into cold water, peel, halve, and remove seeds. Substitute: other grapes, though seedless ones are too small to make a good garnish.

KIDNEYS, CALF'S Quite expensive. Remove the surrounding fat (suet). Soak for 1 hour in milk to remove blood. Rinse, dry and cut in half lengthways. Remove tough core. Slice or dice. Do not overcook; leave slightly pink. Substitute: see next entry.

KIDNEYS, LAMB'S Less expensive but excellent roasted pink in their suet. Roast about 10 minutes in a hot oven, trim off fat and slice thinly.

KOHLRABI Bulbous, mild flavoured root of a variety of cabbage. Purple or green. Peel and use raw in crudités. Substitute: small turnips.

LAMB If you can, choose the fillet or 'eye' from a best end of Welsh lamb. One rack gives 4 portions. Use trimmings for mince. Substitute: New Zealand lamb.

LANGOUSTINES Substitute: king prawns.

LARDONS See Bacon.

LEEKS Where possible, use thin, young leeks. Cut into 2cm [1 inch] lengths, wash well (often very dirty), and blanch for 4 minutes.
JULIENNE: use larger leeks. Substitutes: spring onions or chives.

LEMONS Choose thin skinned lemons for segments or juice. A squeeze of lemon juice in sauces cuts down richness, balances saltiness. Also keeps cut surfaces of fruit from browning.

LIMES More subtle taste than lemons. Use segments quickly once cut, as they lose colour. Substitute: lemons.

LIVER, CALF'S Use Dutch if possible: more expensive but better quality. Remove thin membrane from outside. Cook very quickly to sear outside but leave inside pink. Substitute: lamb's liver.

LOBSTERS Choose Scotch or Cornish for preference. Should be live. Cook as crabs, minimum 10 minutes, plus 10 minutes per kg [5 per lb]. Separate head from tail and claws. Crack claws and remove meat. Use scissors to cut along each side of tail underbody. Remove meat in one piece. Split head, discard greyish sac, and use rest of head and shell for making stocks and sauces. Substitutes: crayfish, langoustines or monkfish tails.

LYCHEES Fruit similar in texture to grapes. Peel off stiff shell and remove single stone. Substitute: canned lychees.

MANGETOUTS Also called sugar or snow peas. Best are small Jersey mangetouts. Only need topping and tailing. Blanch for 1 minute. Reheat in slightly sweetened water, or sprinkle with a little sugar. In crudités: blanch for 30 seconds.

MELONS, CHARENTAIS Small; greyish, netted outside; orange flesh. Very sweet. Scent indicates ripeness. Substitute: cantaloup melons.

MELONS, OGEN Small; green and yellow striped outside; pale green flesh. Very sweet. Scent indicates ripeness. Substitute: Galia melons.

MINT Several species of this herb: grow your favourite outdoors (in a pot, to avoid spreading). Use sparingly in salads and sauces. Freeze as basil.

MONKFISH Usually only the skinned tail is sold. Dense, meaty texture; makes a substitute for the texture of lobster or scallops, but unfortunately not the flavour.

MULLET, RED Pink skinned fish. French nickname 'bécasse de mer' (sea woodcock) because its liver is edible, as is the bird's. Remove scales, but leave skin on.

MUSSELS Best are bouchots from the northern French or Netherlands coast, cleaner and needing less attention than local kinds. Any that are open when bought and will not shut when nudged or tapped are dead: discard them. All should open when cooked: if any do not, discard these too.

MUSHROOMS, CULTIVATED Come in three forms: button, cups and flat. Flat have more flavour but produce more liquid when cooked.

MUSHROOMS, WILD Many recipes here specify wild mushrooms. Larger supermarkets now sometimes have a few kinds. Delicatessens often stock dried European ceps (see below for various names) and dried Chinese or Japanese mushrooms (usually shiitake). Country dwellers can gather their own. Use a good reference book; botanical names are given below. All except morels are autumn species. Substitutes: wild mushrooms of other species, often just as good; or cultivated mushrooms, which have little flavour in comparison, but can be improved by adding some dried ceps.

CEPS (French: *cèpes*/German: *Steinpilze*/ Italian: [*funghi*] *porcini*/ botanical: *Boletus edulis* and other species): found in deciduous and coniferous woods. Brown, shiny cap (other species vary), spongy underside, thick stem. Strong flavour, especially when dried. Fresh: trim away sponge if soggy. Clean well to remove insects. Dried: soak till swollen. Rinse well.

CHANTERELLES (French: *girolles*/ botanical: *Cantharellus cibarius*): found in deciduous woods. Trumpet shape, bright yellow. Occasionally on sale dried. Particularly good in sauces. Do not overcook or their chewy texture becomes tough.

HORNS OF PLENTY (French: *trompettes des morts*/ botanical: *Cratellerus cornucopoides*): found under beech trees. Little, almost black trumpets prized more for their colour than their faint flavour. Sometimes used to fake diced truffle in pâtés.

MORELS (French: *morilles*/botanical: *Morchella esculenta* and other species): found in woods and fields in spring. Cap looks like conical brown sponge, with large holes all over. Delicious, but one of the most expensive fungi to buy. Shape makes them good for stuffing. May be bought canned or dried. Fresh or dried: rinse very well to remove grit.

OYSTER MUSHROOMS (French: *pleurotes*/botanical: *Pleurotus ostreatus*): stemless 'bracket' fungus growing on dying deciduous trees. Grey cap with whitish gills, meaty flavour, edible only when young. Now sold in supermarkets.

WOOD HEDGEHOG MUSHROOMS (French: *pieds de mouton*/botanical: *Hydnum repandum*): found in deciduous woods. Yellowy brown with 'rubber brush' spines instead of gills, needing careful cleaning. Solid, good flavour.

Rarely on sale; expensive.

NASTURTIUM Garden flower, with edible leaves, flowers and seeds. Leaves taste peppery (like watercress, a related plant); good in salads. Flowers make edible decoration. (Seeds formerly used as substitute for capers.)

NETTLES Pick young stinging nettle leaves in countryside (wear gloves). Avoid flowering plants. Discard stems. Nettles are not on sale. Substitutes: spinach or sorrel.

NUTMEG Spice useful for seasoning both savoury and sweet dishes. Buy whole nutmegs and grate as needed.

OILS OLIVE OIL: use first pressing 'extra virgin' oil where its strong flavour is an advantage; and where this is unwanted, rather than inferior olive oil use a refined, deodorized type such as:

PEANUT OIL (groundnut/arachis/ French: *huile d'arachide*).

SESAME OIL: nutty flavour. Becoming more widely available. Substitute: mixture of peanut oil and tahina (sesame paste, from Middle Eastern shops).

WALNUT OIL (French: *huile de noix*) and HAZELNUT OIL (French: *huile de noisettes*) are not widely sold and are expensive, but give excellent nutty flavour in cold and warm salad dressings. Keep refrigerated once opened.

OYSTERS No longer true that these are only edible during months containing the letter R; different kinds are available all year round. Open with special oyster knife. Reserve juice for sauce or poaching liquid. Poach for 30 seconds. Colchester oysters are especially good.

PARTRIDGE Small game bird with pale flesh. Substitutes: any small game bird or guinea fowl.

PASTRY FILO: buy ready made from larger stores and Greek shops. Dries out quickly once opened. Keep well wrapped. Work quickly. Brush each sheet lightly with melted butter. See diagrams on *page 138*.

PUFF AND SHORTCRUST: easier to make than filo, but ready made types are widely available and are usually good.

PEARS I prefer William pears for eating fresh, but choose Comice for poached savoury pear dishes. To 2 litres

[4 pints] water add: juice of 2 lemons/ 1 bay leaf/2 cloves/1 stick cinnamon.

PEPPER, CAYENNE Very hot, orange coloured powder made from chilli peppers: use carefully.

PEPPERCORNS Black, white and green. Use freshly ground black where distinctive peppery taste is required and black specks do not matter. White are hot but less pungent; use in creamy sauces. Green, available canned in brine, are a 'nouvelle cuisine' speciality which I consider overrated. (Pink peppercorns, from a different plant, were a passing fad; now known to be actually poisonous if consumed in large quantities.)

PEPPERS Also called capsicums or pimentos. Green, red, yellow and other colours. Must be firm and shiny; avoid soft or wrinkled ones. Deep fry, grill or put in hot oven till skin blisters. Peel, halve and seed.

PESTO See under Basil.

PIGEONS Where possible choose French corn fed pigeons, tender though expensive; British pigeons are well flavoured but rather tough. Roasted pink, thinly sliced breasts attractive in salads. Substitute: quails.

QUAILS Small birds now raised commercially and even sold ready boned by some poulterers. Others may bone them if asked. Substitutes: any small game or 'baby chickens' (poussins).

QUAIL'S EGGS Tiny eggs taste exactly like hen's eggs; however, their size is a novelty. Substitute: smallest available hen's eggs.

RADICCHIO Usual Italian name for red salad leaf also called 'red lettuce' (actually it's an endive). Bitter, but good used sparingly in salads where it looks most striking. Substitute for flavour only: chicory.

RASPBERRIES Do not wash; it spoils them. Pick over for mouldy fruit and insects. Frozen raspberries are good for sauces.

RAVIOLI If making it yourself, roll out the pasta very thinly. Can be filled with almost anything you fancy. Ready-made fresh ravioli, now widely sold, is usually excellent.

ROQUEFORT Sharp flavoured blue cheese. Nearest substitutes: Pipo Crème and Stilton, but both lack its bite.

SAFFRON Spice made from crocus stamens. Bright yellow colour, unique flavour. Very expensive. If stamens are bought, soak in a little warm water before using them. Substitute for colour only: turmeric.

SALMON Use wild Scotch if possible. Canadian and farmed can be used but have less flavour and lack firmness. Ask fishmonger for fillets rather than cutlets. Substitute: salmon trout.

SCALLOPS Open shell with special knife. Remove sandy sac and rinse well to remove grit. Orange roe, known as coral, delicious used whole, puréed or made into mousse. Scallops and coral can be marinated in seasoned lime or lemon juice and eaten raw. Substitute: monkfish has similar texture, but nothing can duplicate flavour.

SEA BASS One of the best saltwater fish, with a meaty texture. Expensive. Substitute: any firm fleshed white fish.

SEAWEED Type sold by fishmongers as garnish for oysters is not edible (though other kinds are). Blanch for 30 seconds till brilliant green, but not longer or it starts to pop and goes gluey.

SEA URCHINS Spiky, spherical shell contains edible orange roe. Seldom seen in Britain except at specialist fishmongers (and then they have usually been gathered in Ireland, sent to France and re-exported to England!). Ensure loose spines have been removed from inside. Cut flattish top off shell with scissors or special urchin cutter. Drain. Filter juice with sieve, and use in recipe with roes. Rinse shell to use as decorative container.

SHALLOT Small, brown, elongated relative of onion with smoother flavour. Peel and chop very finely for sauces.

SOLE Use Dover sole when affordable. Skin both sides, black and white. Remove 4 fillets. Use bones for stock. Substitute: lemon sole (a kind of dab, not nearly as good).

SPINACH Wash very thoroughly. To use leaves as wrapping: blanch for 30 seconds, dry and pare off central rib.

SWEETBREADS Use calf's sweetbreads for preference. Soak in iced salted water to extract blood. Cook whole in unsalted boiling water for 10 minutes. Leave to cool in liquid. Remove and weight between two plates overnight. Remove gristly bits and as much of the outside film as you can without the sweetbreads falling apart.

Slice or dice. Substitute: lamb's sweetbreads.

THYME Several varieties of this herb, all easy to grow outdoors. Strong flavour. Use tips and small stems, chopped or whole (remove before serving) in stocks and sauces. If old and woody, strip leaves and discard stems. Dries well, or freeze as basil.

TOMATOES Blanch for 10 seconds to loosen skin. If necessary, start peeling by inserting knife tip.

TOMATOES, CHERRY Tiny, sweet, good for garnishing. Peel as ordinary tomatoes. Use whole or halved.

TRUFFLES Best kinds black French and white Alba (Italian); others markedly inferior. Use only the best though appallingly expensive (1984: £200 per kg). Use very sparingly. Peel, save peelings and chop for sauces. Fresh are best but good quality canned available: choose top grade 'primeur cuisson'. Peelings and juice can also be bought in cans. Substitute: 'garnishing paste' in cans is a poor quality alternative without any flavour.

TURBOT Large flat fish, expensive. Fillet, reserve bones for stock. Skin. Substitute: brill.

TURMERIC Powdered spice used as colour substitute for saffron, but flavour is quite different.

TURNIPS Very small, young turnips are good raw in crudités. Peel. Turnip balls make good garnish. Use smallest parisienne cutter. Blanch for 3 minutes.

VEAL Use Dutch milk fed veal fillet: not cheap but very little waste. Substitutes: haunch of veal, or beef or lamb fillet.

VINEGARS Flavoured vinegars can now be bought in many shops. If unavailable, use white or red wine vinegar.

WATERCRESS Wash very well to remove small slugs or snails. Blanch for 20 seconds.

WOODCOCK Small, delicate game bird. Should not be allowed to become too high. Cooked and served undrawn: liver and other entrails considered a delicacy (but gizzard must be discarded). Substitutes: quail or snipe.

GLOSSARY OF COOKING TECHNIQUES AND EQUIPMENT

ACIDULATED WATER Water with a little vinegar or lemon juice added. Used to cover cut fruits or vegetables to prevent browning, and for poaching eggs to stop the white from spreading.

BAIN-MARIE Used for very gentle cooking of delicate foods and sauces. Food is put in a container above or in a pan of warm water, and so heated indirectly. The same can be done in an oven by standing a dish in a pan of water, which protects from the intensity of direct heat.

BASTE To spoon fat or cooking liquids over foods during cooking in order to keep them moist.

BLANC Mixture used to preserve colour of white or pale vegetables during cooking. Mix 25g [1oz] flour with 3 tbsp water. Add to 1 litre [2 pints] water. Mix well. Pass through fine sieve. Season. Add juice of 1 lemon and 75g [3oz] unsalted butter.

BLANCH To cook vegetables for a short time in boiling water or a blanc. Purpose may be to remove bitterness; to soften slightly; to loosen skins for peeling; and to intensify colour. Blanching times are given wherever appropriate. Use large pan with plenty of salted water (or blanc). Bring to boil. Add vegetables. Leave pan uncovered. Bring back to boil: time from this moment. When time is up, remove vegetables and at once plunge them into bowl of iced water to arrest cooking.

BLENDER See Food processor.

CLARIFY To clear of solids or impurities. Clarified butter resists burning at high temperatures. Melt butter gently. Leave to stand for a few minutes. Pour slowly through fine muslin, leaving sediment in pan. Keeps very well in the refrigerator.

COURT-BOUILLON Cooking water flavoured, as by adding stock.

DEGLAZE To add a liquid to a pan after frying or roasting to loosen the tasty residue. The mixture can then be used as basis for a sauce.

DICE To cut into small cubes.

EMULSIFY To form an emulsion, the blending of an oily with a watery liquid.

Milk is a natural emulsion; mayonnaise is one you make. Emulsions are unstable and liable to separate.

FLATTEN To beat a fillet of fish or meat with a mallet until extremely thin. It can then be shaped into an envelope or container for filling.

FOLD To combine delicate ingredients such as whipped cream or egg whites, where stirring or beating would destroy the foam. Use a large metal spoon. Lift one substance and turn it gently over the other, repeating until the two are more or less mixed: blending totally would also destroy the delicate structure of the foam.

FOOD PROCESSOR AND LIQUIDIZER (BLENDER) Most of the recipes in this book allow the use of either machine. Sometimes a food processor gives a slightly coarser result. If so, pass the food through a sieve.

JULIENNE To cut into fine strips; the result is also called a julienne.

LARD To thread a strip of an ingredient through meat or fish. Larding needles are sold for the purpose. Generally larding is done with strips of fat, to moisten food; but in this book it is done with truffle and salmon strips for decorative effect.

LIQUIDIZER See Food processor.

MARINATE To soak meat or fish in a marinade, a liquid mixture that moistens and flavours it. Marinades containing acid ingredients such as vinegar or lemon juice, or certain fresh fruit juices which contain natural enzymes, tenderize meat and act on fish in the same way as cooking.

MEDALLION Small circular slice.

PARISIENNE CUTTER Scoop for making balls of fruits or vegetables. There are various sizes.

PIPE To force a mixture through the nozzle of a forcing bag. Done to create decorative effects, often using a fancy nozzle; or as a means of filling hollow items.

POACH To cook gently in simmering water, acidulated water or court-bouillon. Soft-poached eggs: tip out of shells directly into acidulated water. Cook until white hardens but yolk remains soft. Remove with slotted spoon. Plunge directly into iced water to arrest cooking. The fresher the eggs, the better the results.

REDUCE To boil a liquid to evaporate the water content, concentrating flavour and consistency.

SAUTÉ To cook in a shallow pan with butter or oil over a fast heat. This seals the outside of the food, thereby retaining the juices inside.

SEED To remove seeds. Usually done to improve presentation rather than flavour; but it makes tomatoes less watery.

SKIN To remove skin. Often done for appearance only. However, skins of tomatoes and some other vegetables may be indigestible and bitter, and are best removed. Instructions are given where appropriate.

STEAM To cook above a boiling or simmering liquid, in a steamer or bain-marie. The top section of the pan must be well fitting and covered to keep the steam in.

SWEAT To cook over a low heat, usually in butter or oil, causing juices to run out of food and softening it. Salt may be added to help extract the liquid.

INDEX

Main references are given first in roman type. Italic numerals indicate recipes in which the item appears.